P9-DDV-273

THE WALL STREET JOURNAL.

COMPLETE REAL-ESTATE INVESTING GUIDEBOOK

OTHER BOOKS FROM
THE WALL STREET JOURNAL.

The Wall Street Journal. Guide to the Business of Life
Nancy Keates

The Wall Street Journal. Complete Money & Investing Guidebook
Dave Kansas

The Wall Street Journal. Complete Personal Finance Guidebook
Jeff D. Opdyke

The Wall Street Journal. Complete Personal Finance Workbook
Jeff D. Opdyke

The Wall Street Journal. Complete Identity Theft Guidebook
Terri Cullen

THE WALL STREET JOURNAL.

COMPLETE REAL-ESTATE INVESTING GUIDEBOOK

DAVID CROOK

THREE RIVERS PRESS

NEW YORK

Copyright © 2006 by Dow Jones & Company

The Wall Street Journal® is a registered trademark of Dow Jones and is used by permission.

All rights reserved.
Published in the United States by Three Rivers Press, an imprint of the Crown Publishing Group, a division of Random House, Inc., New York.
www.crownpublishing.com

THREE RIVERS PRESS and the Tugboat design are registered trademarks of Random House, Inc.

Grateful acknowledgement is made to the following for permission to use illustrations: p. 8, © 2006 Larry Jones c/o the ispot.com; p. 22, © 2006 Jay Belmore c/o theispot.com; p. 28, © 2006 Adam McCauley c/o theispot.com; p. 46, © 2006 Richard Downs c/o theispot.com; p. 65, © 2006 Mitch Frey c/o theispot.com; p. 75, © 2006 Riccardo Stampatori c/o theispot.com; p. 84, © 2006 John Kachik c/o theispot.com; p. 113, © 2006 John S. Dykes Collection c/o theispot.com; p. 127, © 2006 Peter Hoey c/o theispot.com; p. 148, © 2006 Michael Witte c/o theispot.com; p. 168, © 2006 James Steinberg c/o theispot.com; p. 179, © 2006 John Kachik c/o theispot.com.

Library of Congress Cataloging-in-Publication Data

Crook, David, 1953–
The Wall Street Journal complete real-estate investing guidebook / David Crook.—1st ed.
Includes bibliographical references.
1. Real-estate investment.   I. Title.
HD1382.5.C76 2006
332.63'24—dc22   2006023160

ISBN 978-0-307-34562-2

Printed in the United States of America

Design by Mauna Eichner and Lee Fukui

20 19 18 17 16 15 14 13 12 11

First Edition

CONTENTS

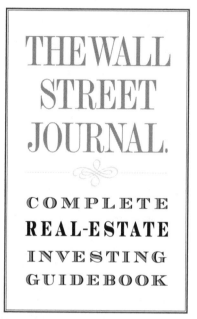

THE WALL STREET JOURNAL.

COMPLETE
REAL-ESTATE
INVESTING
GUIDEBOOK

INTRODUCTION
SO YOU WANT TO BE A
MILLIONAIRE?

*This land is your land and this land is my land—sure—but
the world is run by those that never listen to music anyway.*
—BOB DYLAN

This book is for people who want to make money investing in real estate.

Hucksters and schemers use dubious investment books and middle-of-the-night TV shows to peddle hundreds of real-estate schemes to a gullible public. They promise no-work shortcuts to wealth and "financial freedom" as they reveal the moneymaking "secrets" that real-estate professionals keep from you and everyone else. They say they'll show you how to "flip your way to financial success" or "renovate for riches." Some claim they'll show you how to build multimillion-dollar empires with no money, no experience and no skills.

Enough already. These are the fantasies of losers. And if that is what you expect from a book about real-estate investing, here is the best advice you will get from this one: Don't buy it. You don't need to waste any more of your money.

If, however, you recognize that real-estate investing, like all investing, is more marathon than sprint and that the only person to get rich quickly in a get-rich-quick scheme is the other guy, then by all means buy this book. It's not the only real-estate investing book you'll ever need, it's the first one.

And let's start by exploring the uncertain but promising future for today's new real-estate investors.

Real estate has demonstrated itself time after time to be a proven path to building and preserving wealth. The first multimillionaire in U.S. history, John Jacob Astor, built a fortune that survived 200 years by reinvesting his fur-trading profits in New York City real estate. Today, real estate and real-estate-related businesses are major components in the portfolios of nearly a quarter of the men and women on the Forbes 400 list of the wealthiest Americans.

No one's suggesting here that you can join the billionaire's club with a few rental properties. But even a modestly successful real-estate investor should be able to amass a seven-figure fortune. You can have a good home, educate your children, contribute to the community, live a comfortable retirement and pass along a substantial estate.

That's how real-estate investing has worked for most of the last seven decades. Since the end of World War II, the United States has enjoyed a remarkable run-up in the value of housing and other real estate. Firm numbers don't exist, but various sources suggest that the total value of U.S. real estate could approach an unfathomable $45 trillion, roughly half in the hands of private individuals and families.

Such a vast, democratic accumulation of wealth would be beyond the dreams of the GIs, the small landlords and the shopkeepers who launched the United States on its broad path of property ownership. They probably didn't look much farther than their own property lines as they slowly built the bases of their family fortunes.

The population grew, the number of households grew, family income grew, all fueling the historic shift of homes, offices and factories from the cities to the suburbs. A generous national government subsidized the acquisition of real estate as it encouraged development of cheap land and assured a plentiful supply of cheap gasoline. The nation was transformed, for good and bad. It became a place quite different from where our grandparents and great-grandparents grew up.

Throughout this period of remarkably sustained prosperity, property and home values—reflecting most families' principal assets—rose just enough ahead of inflation to defy financial history and gravity. Indeed, for the half century that preceded the post–World War II boom, the trend in home prices was just as predictably downward. Housing, compared to the cost of living, was cheaper in 1940 than in 1900.

Such a decline was unimaginable through the postwar run-up, however. Prices skyrocketed right after the war and then maintained their steady inflation-plus ride for decades. Parts of the country experienced periodic real-estate manias, most notably in the late 1970s, again in the late 1980s and the early 2000s.

Real-estate prices rose so much that houses became essential components of the middle-class's wealth-building, college-funding and retirement plans.

Modestly well-to-do home sellers who bought and held could count on sending their children to elite private universities and funding their own carefree 30-year retirements in the gated golf-and-tennis communities of the Sunbelt. They'd sell their Bethesda, Lake Forest, Mineola, Palo Alto or Garden Grove houses to panicky buyers convinced that they, too, had to "get into" the real-estate market before prices rose even more, before their dreams of home ownership and their own comfortable 30-year retirements would pass forever beyond their means.

These manias were usually followed by eras, well, less manic. Prices rarely declined—though they did in Texas in the 1980s and in New England and Southern California in the 1990s—but instead settled down for a while. There were fewer frantic buyers, and sellers stopped asking for ever higher prices.

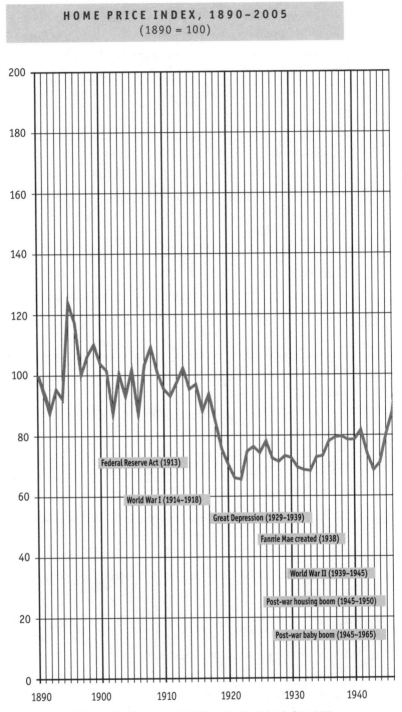

HOME PRICE INDEX, 1890–2005
(1890 = 100)

Federal Reserve Act (1913)

World War I (1914–1918)

Great Depression (1929–1939)

Fannie Mae created (1938)

World War II (1939–1945)

Post-war housing boom (1945–1950)

Post-war baby boom (1945–1965)

Source: Robert J. Shiller, Irrational Exuberance, 2nd Edition, Princeton University Press, 2005

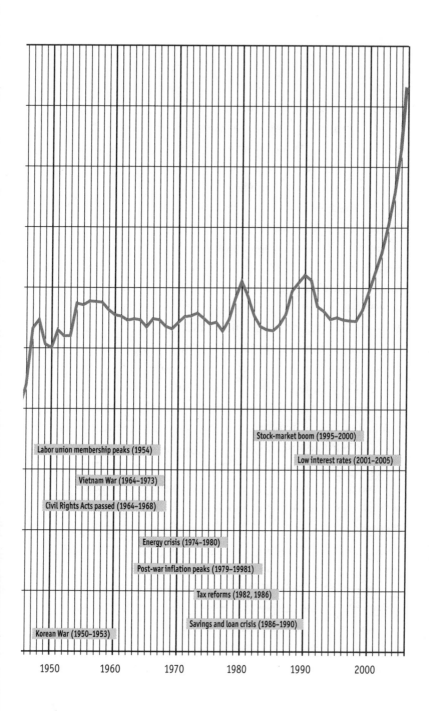

Labor union membership peaks (1954)

Stock-market boom (1995–2000)

Low interest rates (2001–2005)

Vietnam War (1964–1973)

Civil Rights Acts passed (1964–1968)

Energy crisis (1974–1980)

Post-war inflation peaks (1979–19981)

Tax reforms (1982, 1986)

Savings and loan crisis (1986–1990)

Korean War (1950–1953)

1950   1960   1970   1980   1990   2000

But long-term homeowners always seemed to muddle through unscathed. And before you knew it, something clicked in the country, and buyers' real-estate passions were fired anew.

We are now coming to the end of the greatest mania of the era. In the big metropolitan areas on the coasts, house prices rose far faster than inflation and, even more significantly for real-estate investors, faster than rents. In his widely read and debated book *Irrational Exuberance*, Yale University economist Robert J. Shiller demonstrated that in the years after the bursting of the Internet stock bubble in 2000, home prices rose dangerously fast and high, mimicking the sharp run-up of NASDAQ technology stocks in the late 1990s.

By the summer of 2006, it was clear that the great boom was coming to an end. Rising interest rates, outlandish prices and escalating energy costs were coming together to thwart property investors. We can only hope that the inevitable comedown of prices doesn't mimic the NASDAQ, too.

Whatever the coming year or two may bring—whether a soft landing for real-estate prices, a crash or even the start of a long, relentless Japan-style decline—real-estate investors face a challenging financial environment. The quick money's been made. The future is most likely going to belong to the well-financed buy-and-hold crowd, either those who had acquired their properties by the mid-1990s, before the prices started accelerating, or those who have picked up distressed properties as the bubble has deflated. In a long, slow decline, however, even properties bought for just 70 percent or 60 percent of their previous high values could end up looking expensive as selling prices fall even further.

In any case, prudence would suggest that modern investors should not expect to rely on ever-rising real-estate prices to make up for bad deal making and management failures. Annual price increases of 20 percent or 30 percent can paper over a lot of mistakes. Stagnant or falling values will uncover them.

This is a period for conservative, thoughtful, thrifty investors, not for erstwhile swashbucklers and certainly not for dreamers who think they can get something for next to nothing. But there are still fortunes to be made in real estate. There are still multimillionaires to be born and family fortunes to be built.

REAL-ESTATE SECRETS REVEALED

Here's what real-estate hucksters really don't want you to know: The "secrets" of real-estate investing are not particularly hard to divine. Anyone can learn how to make money in real estate because, as in most finance, the basics of real-estate investing are fairly easy to figure out.

- **Buy a property for less than you can sell it.**

- **Use as much of other people's money as you can.**

- **Make sure your property pays for itself.**

- **Take maximum advantage of the tax laws.**

That's it. That's all you need to know to build a real-estate fortune. Do that with every property you have, and you will be successful. You could even become a millionaire . . . but given today's real-estate prices, you should do far better than that.

Throughout this book, we will be expanding on and illuminating those basic rules of real-estate investing. In chapter 1, **"Your Home Is *Not* an Investment Property,"** we'll set straight the number one misconception that most Americans have about real-estate investing. We'll demonstrate the fundamental differences between buying a house and investing in income properties, and show why most homeowners sorely misunderstand the finances that underpin their most valuable asset.

FIRST THINGS FIRST

 Although this is not a general investing guide, it's impossible to get started without addressing a couple of broad personal-finance issues. Like all investing, real-estate investing requires financial discipline, short-term sacrifices and a long-term commitment. Before you start:

Stop spending so much. If your credit cards aren't at zero balance and you don't have more money saved at the end of the year than you had at the beginning, it is because you are spending too much. Cut out restaurants, your morning Grande at Starbucks, cable TV, cell phones, ballet lessons, poker night—whatever it takes to get your expenses below your income. Then use your savings to make more money for yourself and your family.

Save as much as you can in tax-deferred retirement accounts. Always be sure to put at least enough in your 401(k) to get your employer's full match—it's the only guaranteed 100 percent return on your money that exists. Put in more if you can. If you can open a tax-deferred IRA, a Roth IRA or any other similar retirement account for you or your spouse, do it.

Don't confuse purchases with investments. Purchases cost you money; investments make you money. Don't delude yourself that jewelry, couture fashions, automobiles, sports memorabilia, porcelain figurines, art prints or any other collectibles are investments that someday will be worth a fortune. They won't. Few such items, if any, will increase in value in your or your children's lifetimes. If you want to leave something to your heirs, buy bonds—not Beanie Babies.

If you don't pay attention to these rules before you try to jump into the real-estate market, you will be hard-pressed to make much money at it. You will be forever playing catch-up. You will never get ahead financially. And you will never do more than dream of what you might have built if you had just gotten that one lucky break or won the lottery.

By all means, make use of your lucky breaks—an unexpected bonus, an inheritance—but recognize that lucky breaks, by definition, come along only once in a while. And you already know that you probably won't ever win the lottery. So it's better to take charge of your own financial life rather than wait around for fate to do it for you.

In chapter 2, "**Getting In on the Ground Floor: Where to Get the Money and Build a Network for Investing in Real Estate,**" we will explore how to raise the money you will need to get started and show you how to find the people who can help you become a real-estate investor. As the title of chapter 3 says, "**The Three Questions**" will ask—and show you how to answer— the most fundamental questions that every investor must ask about every property.

Then, in chapter 4, "**Finding, Buying and Closing the Deal,**" we'll walk through the process of finding and valuing properties. We'll go through the basics of real-estate finance and take you up to the point when you are ready to close a deal on your first property.

Next, in chapter 5, "**Why the IRS Is Your Friend,**" you'll see how the government blesses real-estate investors with tax breaks and loopholes that salaried workers and even stocks-and-bonds investors can only wish for. You will also see how phantom "paper" losses in real estate can be used to reduce taxes on your salary income.

Then we zero in on how you can get into real estate with relatively little money by buying smaller types of investment properties, starting at the bottom of the real-estate investing food chain in chapter 6, "**There's No Place Like a Home: Smaller Residential Investment Properties,**" and heading all the way up to huge regional shopping centers that cost hundreds of millions of dollars to build and hundreds of millions more to operate in chapter 7, "**Going Commercial: Larger Apartment Complexes and Commercial Buildings.**"

This book is about real-estate *investing*—the financial aspects of acquiring and operating and selling properties. But in chapter 8, "**Do You Really Want to Be a Landlord?**" we'll discuss some of the nuts-and-bolts business of being a landlord, the job that most distinguishes real-estate investing from stocks, bonds or other investments.

But we'll get into those in chapter 9, "**Real Estate on Wall Street: REITs,**" where we will look at some of the hands-off investments that you can make in the real-estate sector in the traditional stock-and-bond markets.

Finally, in chapter 10, "**Are You Rich Yet? The 20 Things Every Real-Estate Investor Needs to Know,**" we'll review the big points and get ready for the finish, where I'll reveal the one and only guaranteed path to wealth and financial freedom. (No peeking!)

Despite the emphasis on finance, you won't see a great deal of arithmetic. The legal language is kept within reason, too. There are bits of both, but nothing will make your head hurt because everything in this book is written for novice real-estate investors.

After all, an experienced real-estate investor probably doesn't need this book. But even a sophisticated stock investor may be unfamiliar with the intricacies of real-estate finance. And no one would expect a hedge-fund manager to know much about plumbing—though once you become a landlord, what you don't know about plumbing could end up costing you a lot more than what you don't know about derivatives.

Nothing about real-estate investing or ownership is automatically assumed, not even that you already own your own home.

Indeed, it might be a good thing if you don't already have a house, for the first and most important lesson of property investing addresses the great misunderstanding that most Americans have about real estate.

CHAPTER 1

YOUR HOME IS *NOT* AN INVESTMENT PROPERTY

"Land is the only thing in the world that amounts to anything . . . for 'tis the only thing in this world that lasts. . . . 'Tis the only thing worth working for, worth fighting for—worth dying for."

— MARGARET MITCHELL

Your home is a lot of things, most of them good. Your home is your castle, your refuge, your escape. It may be the physical manifestation of all your material hopes and aspirations, your piece of the American dream. It gives comfort and protection to you and your family. It may be an essential part of your retirement or college-savings plans. Your home is probably your biggest asset, and the price you could ask for it today is almost certainly higher than the price you paid for it back whenever.

But your home is not an investment property.

Investing in real estate isn't the same as owning a house. If you don't get anything else out of this book, you need to understand that—especially now that so many homeowners are trying to play the real-estate game with their homes. That's dangerous—not because the value of your home is likely to decline (though it could), but because you are more likely to spend far more money living in your home than you will make when you sell it.

Investing is investing. It's using your money to make more money. Anything else, including most home purchases, is spending.

To be considered investments, real-estate purchases must generate actual profits, either immediately in the form of income or long-term in the form of appreciation. In either case, the property must cover all its own costs and produce a reasonable return on the money you spent to buy it.

You will read and hear other terms for measuring investment income—rate of return, "cap rate," net operating income, rental roll. Each is different, but one way or another, they all come down to the most basic concept of real-estate investing: "cash flow"—real in-your-pocket-put-it-in-the-bank money that's left over after you have covered all your business expenses. That's something you don't get when you just own a home. Yes, your house is a huge asset. But without cash flow, you might as well be holding on to a very big, very expensive Beanie Baby.

You are thinking I'm nuts. You're saying, "I bought my house in 1990 for $200,000. I put in a thousand-square-foot addition, including a new bathroom. I redid the old bathroom and put in a new kitchen and a deck with a hot tub. I could get $650,000 for it today."

That sure sounds like an investment. But if you run the numbers, you will see that it's not much of an investment at all. How would you feel about a stock that cost you more to own than you make when you sell it?

Take a look at this spreadsheet, which represents 16 years of ownership of a house in the Los Angeles area. We're sticking to simple concepts and round numbers here. But with a few assumptions—including the improvements, regular main-

		YOUR HOME IS NOT AN INVESTMENT PROPERTY			
Year	Total Value	Mortgage Debt*	Annual Costs**	Profit/ (Loss)	
BUY	$200,000	($160,000)			
1990	$200,000	($160,000)	($20,385)		8.5% mortgage
1991	$210,000	($157,600)	($15,385)		
1992	$220,500	($155,200)	($15,385)		
1993	$266,525	($202,800)	($18,936)		Kitchen ($50,000); refinance at 7.5%
1994	$279,851	($200,400)	($17,436)		
1995	$293,844	($198,000)	($32,436)		Paint job ($15,000)
1996	$308,536	($195,600)	($17,436)		
1997	$323,963	($193,200)	($17,436)		
1998	$340,161	($190,800)	($18,615)		Refinance (6.5%)
1999	$357,169	($188,400)	($15,615)		
2000	$375,027	($186,000)	($15,615)		
2001	$393,779	($183,600)	($15,615)		
2002	$413,468	($181,200)	($40,615)		New roof ($25,000)
2003	$434,141	($178,800)	($15,615)		
2004	$560,848	($326,400)	($27,433)		Addition ($150,000); refinance at 5.75%
2005	$588,891	($324,000)	($22,933)		
2006	$618,335	($321,600)	($87,933)		
SELL	$650,000	($321,600)	($414,824)	($86,424)	

*Includes additional borrowing to finance improvements.

**Includes after-tax mortgage payments, maintenance, financing and sales costs.

tenance and a couple of big ticket repairs such as a paint job and a new roof—this typical homeowner actually loses more than $5,000 a year, even as the house "appreciates" at a steady and optimistic 5 percent annually. Put simply: At the end of the 16 years of ownership, this home seller will have spent $415,000 in order to pocket $328,000—a loss of $86,000.

How is that possible? When homeowners compute their returns, they rarely consider all the costs of owning a property. Generally, they don't do much more than subtract their down payment—$40,000 in this case—from the proceeds of the sale ($328,000) and declare they made a huge "profit" ($288,000).

But it doesn't really work that way. There are big problems with this typical homeowner's investment plan.

Homeowners rarely consider maintenance or the declining value of improvements. Painting, roof repairs or new furnaces don't pay for themselves, and remodeling is a huge loser. Entire industries have arisen to entice homeowners to spend thousands of dollars for new kitchen cabinets, granite countertops and stainless-steel appliances or his-and-hers master suite bathroom spas featuring multihead showers and Asian-inspired "soaking" tubs. Architects, builders, magazine editors and real-estate agents tout such improvements as if typical homeowners absolutely must take the remodeling plunge or forever risk the value of the house and suffer the ridicule of friends and neighbors.

Remodeling magazine publishes a widely quoted annual survey of the value of home improvements. In 2005, the magazine said that an upscale kitchen remodel like you see in the glossy shelter magazines would cost $82,000 and would return just 84 percent four years later. Absurd. This kind of project might get raves from your friends, but it's a fool's financial play. A new kitchen is certainly a nice thing to have, but it's not an investment that's going to make you any money. That 84 percent return means the homeowner will lose more than $3,000 a year on the kitchen. And if the owner borrows the money to remodel the kitchen—which most do—the losses could quickly triple.

That's because long-term borrowing is the home investor's nemesis. How ironic. The 30-year mortgage—which greatly reduced monthly payments and put home ownership within the grasp of nearly 70 percent of American households—locked those same households into Grand Canyons of debt. Mortgage interest, even after the government's mortgage-interest tax-deduction subsidy, is the homeowner's overwhelmingly largest expense, and it drives up the cost of a house so much that a true profit is all but impossible for most owners. In this scenario, the homeowners spent about $234,000 of after-tax money on interest—more than half the total appreciation— over the 16 years. And most Americans move after just 5 to 7 years!

Adding further insult: You can't spend a home—or even a new kitchen. No matter that the increased value of the house is pushing up the owners' net worth—they can only borrow against their house or sell it. If they borrow, they are digging themselves another debt hole. In order to make the debt worth taking on, they'd have to forgo the new kitchen and invest the proceeds of the loan in something that will return more than it costs to pay the interest and the principal. Just to break even, then, the homeowner who borrows for 30 years at 6.5 percent would need to invest that $82,000 in something that would return at least $6,200 a year. As you will learn from this book, a good place to invest might be a rental property. But certainly not in a new kitchen.

And if homeowners do choose to sell, they will still have to find a place to live. When home prices rise, they rise in the entire area. So if the homeowners stay in the same metropolitan region, they will most likely have to move to a much smaller house or to a less-desirable neighborhood or take out another mortgage and restart the debt clock.

Even if they move to a cheaper housing market (and just about any place is cheaper than the Los Angeles area), they are likely to spend most or all of their cash on their new house. Again, the return is pretty much an illusion. That $328,000 will buy a very nice place in Las Vegas, Phoenix, Boise or some of the other cities of the West overflowing with former Californians. But at what real cost?

Now in their 50s or 60s and living mortgage free, these Equity Ex-Pats will be leaving their heirs some property. But as investors, they have been net losers. In this example, they will have paid nearly $750,000 to buy that new house—you have to add the $415,000 they spent on the first house to get the $328,000 they paid for the new house. And they must still pay and keep paying to maintain the new house and to cover taxes and insurance.

To be fair, homeowners have to live somewhere, and they have to pay rent to someone. So they may as well buy and pay "deductible" rent in the form of a mortgage payment. After all, the government does cover a quarter to one-third of mortgage interest through the home-mortgage-interest tax deduction. No renter gets that kind of break. And a homeowner gets the added benefit of enforced savings in that he is paying some principal and the property is appreciating over time.

That's all true, and the "imputed rent" (money that would have been spent on rent but wasn't) that comes from paying for a house with a long-term mortgage is the number one cost savings for homeowners. In this example, a renter living in the same house over the same 16 years could easily pay monthly rents totaling $600,000. In that sense, the homeowner sees a sizable "profit" even as he or she loses thousands of dollars a year on the primary investment. Of course, from a financial perspective, it's not really a profit at all. It's just money that the homeowner did not spend, just as you don't make a $50,000 profit when you choose to buy a $30,000 Buick instead of an $80,000 Mercedes-Benz.

Now if someone feels it's worth more than a half-million dollars to live in this house, who are you to disagree? I'm sure you'll agree as well that it's far better to be receiving that money than to be paying it. So let's look at the same house from a landlord's perspective.

Take a look at this next spreadsheet.

As you can see, even with increasing the annual costs and computing the mortgage interest before, not after, taxes, a

A RENTAL PROPERTY CAN BE A GREAT INVESTMENT

Year	Total Value	Mortgage Debt*	Annual Costs**	Rental Income	Profit/ (Loss)	
BUY	$200,000	($160,000)				
1990	$200,000	($160,000)	($27,656)	$18,000	($9,656)	8.5% mortgage
1991	$210,000	($157,600)	($22,656)	$18,900	($3,756)	
1992	$220,500	($155,200)	($22,656)	$25,845	$3,189	
1993	$266,525	($202,800)	($27,180)	$27,137	($43)	Kitchen ($50,000); refinance at 7.5%
1994	$279,851	($200,400)	($25,680)	$28,494	$2,814	
1995	$293,844	($198,000)	($40,680)	$29,919	($10,761)	Paint job ($15,000)
1996	$308,536	($195,600)	($25,680)	$31,415	$5,735	
1997	$323,963	($193,200)	($25,680)	$32,985	$7,305	
1998	340,161	($190,800)	($26,004)	$34,635	$8,631	Refinance (6.5%)
1999	$357,169	($188,400)	($23,004)	$36,367	$13,363	
2000	$375,027	($186,000)	($23,004)	$38,185	$15,181	
2001	$393,779	($183,600)	($23,004)	$40,094	$17,090	
2002	$413,468	($181,200)	($48,004)	$42,099	($5,905)	New roof ($25,000)
2003	$434,141	($178,800)	($23,004)	$44,204	$21,200	
2004	$560,848	($326,400)	($39,180)	$58,414	$19,234	Addition ($150,000); refinance at 5.75%
2005	$588,891	($324,000)	($34,680)	$61,335	$26,655	
2006	$618,335	($321,600)	($99,680)	$64,401	($35,279)	
SELL	$650,000	($321,600)	($557,432)	$632,429	$403,397	

*Includes additional borrowing to finance improvements.

**Includes before-tax mortgage payments, maintenance, financing and sales costs; excludes depreciation.

landlord makes a handsome profit on the same property that was a financial drain on a homeowner.

The "Profit/(Loss)" column shows how much money the landlord has after paying all his pretax expenses. A nasty negative cash flow in the first year was quickly converted to profits in later years, and the landlord was in the black after just two years. By the last year, the homeowner's money pit had become an ATM handing over more than $2,000 a month to its landlord while actually appreciating at the 5 percent per year rate that the homeowner thought he was getting. (You will see later how the landlord actually does better because of tax laws that favor real-estate investing even more than homeowning.)

Let's take this calculation one step further and put it in terms most people who have a basic familiarity with investing can appreciate. How does this real-estate investment compare with the Dow Jones Industrial Average—the most widely quoted stock-market benchmark?

A $40,000 investment in an index fund tracking the Dow from January 1, 1990, to June 30, 2005—a period when the Dow rose about 273 percent and total return, including stock dividends, was 436 percent—would be worth about $174,400 today, before taxes. So that's our benchmark. Any investor could have done that. So for the sake of this discussion, let's say a reasonable criterion for a successful real-estate venture is to beat the Dow.

We know what happened to the homeowner: a loss of $86,000. That's why a home isn't an investment.

But how good of an investment was the house for our Los Angeles landlord? How well did he do? Outstanding. He had an overall pretax return of $403,000—annual rental income and a hefty profit from the sale of the property.

That's almost two and a half times what he could have done in the stock market, and probably enough to buy a very nice place alongside all the other former Californians in Phoenix, Las Vegas or Boise.

CHAPTER 2

GETTING IN ON THE GROUND FLOOR

WHERE TO GET THE MONEY AND BUILD A NETWORK FOR INVESTING IN REAL ESTATE

"I feel that in a small way we're doing something important. It's satisfying a fundamental urge. It's deep in the race for a man to want his own roof and walls and fireplace. And we're helping him get those things in our shabby little office."

— IT'S A WONDERFUL LIFE

Everyone has to live somewhere. And everyone has to work somewhere. And everyone has to shop somewhere. And someone has to provide the space.

That's where the real-estate investor comes in. He or she is the person who makes money by providing one of life's necessities, just like the water company or the gas company or the

electric utility. And like those lackluster, steady, boring businesses, real-estate investing—properly and prudently done—
can provide considerable wealth and a good income. And
unlike those other businesses, anyone can do it. The capital requirements to get started in real-estate investing are quite minimal, and there are comparatively few legal restrictions on how
you operate.

Keep that in mind throughout this and the next couple of
chapters, because we are now going to look at how you go
about acquiring properties—how to raise money, how to learn
the real-estate business, how you find properties, how to evaluate them from a financial perspective and how you buy them.
There are a lot of broad concepts here—and some simple
math—that will get you through the process.

Don't be discouraged or think for a moment that this is all
too complicated. But do give yourself plenty of time; you should
plan on at least one full year from the time you decide to get
into real-estate investing and when you close on your first
property. Most of that time will be spent educating yourself,
first about investing and real estate in general, and then specifically in neighborhoods and individual properties.

So let's start at the beginning, with the first thing every investor asks.

"WHERE WILL I GET THE MONEY?"

What? You say your trust-fund check didn't come this month?

Join the club. Few Americans have any significant wealth.
The median household net worth in the United States is just
about $55,000—that's what's left when you subtract the debts
from the assets of the family that's financially halfway between
Bill Gates and a homeless person. That includes retirement accounts, savings, home equity, furniture, cars, boats, clothes—
everything. Median financial wealth, which includes only stocks,
bonds, life insurance, cash and the like, is just $28,000.

Most people work hard for a salary that never seems quite

enough after taxes, rent or mortgage payments, car notes, medical bills, groceries, gasoline and whatever else has to be paid each month.

There's not a lot of room there for investing. Most know you should be saving for retirement and your kids' college. But you can barely afford to invest in your company's 401(k). Where can you get the money it takes to get into real estate?

You may already have much of it, and you can get the rest. Clean up your personal finances; get your household expenses under control. Pay off your credit cards. Save some money.

You will need a modest amount of your own capital and access to lenders or other sources of money. Remember: It's called capitalism.

Starter investment properties can be bought under the same easy-lending terms that you can use to buy any residential

A YEAR OF LEARNING, THINKING AND DOING REAL ESTATE

1–3 Months	4–6 Months	7–9 Months	10–12 Months
Educate yourself: Read real-estate investing books; real-estate licensing classes.	**Get the business going:** Interview banks, money sources; work with attorney to set up partnership or corporate entities.	**Get liquid:** Make sure your start-up funds will be available when you need them.	**Go for it:** When you find just the right property, make a solid offer and get going.
Network: Get to know other landlords, real-estate professionals through local clubs and groups.	**Walk the streets:** Get to know the areas you're interested in; talk to local renters and businesspeople, real-estate agents.	**Go shopping:** Take your property visits up a notch; make lowball offers to get a feel for negotiating.	**Do the work:** Financial due diligence and thorough property inspection.
Clean up your personal finances: Pay off any credit-card debts, other creditors; review, correct credit reports, etc.	**Check out properties:** Visit individual properties to get a feel for the market; crunch numbers.	**Get financing preliminaries out of the way:** Get preapproved for loans, have financial papers in order.	**Get your money:** Include financials in loan package; apply.

IRA OR NOT?

Although conventional personal-finance advice discourages the use of IRA funds to buy a house, there are compelling reasons to go the IRA route with an investment property that is also your home. You're simply transferring your funds from one tax-deferred investment vehicle to another, even more favorable one.

You will have to pay taxes on the $10,000 that you take out of your IRA, but you will be investing the money in income-producing property—not just a home. Then, because the property is also your home, you will be allowed to take up to $500,000 profit (if you're married filing jointly) tax free when you sell it. If in the future you move and keep the building as a rental property, you will be allowed to sell it and buy a new rental property, again tax free.

This is a special case that applies only to "first-home" purchases. As you will see in chapter 10, an IRA is not a good way for most people to buy or hold property investments.

※

property. You can get good-quality loans on buildings with up to four apartments in them with as little as a 3 percent down payment (that's just $12,000 on a $400,000 building). It will take a family earning the median national income and saving 10 percent a year just about two and a half years to save that much money.

And Uncle Sam will give you a little help. If you save your money in an IRA, the government will let you take out up to $10,000 penalty free to buy a first home, which could be a small residential building that you share with tenants whose rents will help you buy your property. (The term "first home" is a loose one. If you haven't owned a home for two years, the IRS considers any house you buy a "first home.")

If you are putting together a good deal that shows promise and profits, the rest of the money needn't be especially hard to get, either. A lender will allow you to include the rental income along with your salary when you compute whether you can afford the loan. It's always good to have someone else helping you out with your monthly bills. Try to keep the basic payment—called "PITI" for principal, interest, taxes, insurance—to 25 percent or less of your before-tax income, including the rental income.

You want to limit your risk and you want to buy as much property as you can comfortably afford. You do that by using "leverage"—paying a fraction of the purchase price yourself and borrowing the rest to acquire and operate your properties. It's called using other people's money. It's a good kind of debt to take on if you have an investment that uses even more of other people's money—renters—to make the monthly payments and produce a profit.

Recognize that investment opportunities exist in every city, even on the high-priced coasts. Every city has properties for sale that can be bought for well below their potential values. And remember: That incredibly high "median" price you read about most often in real-estate news stories means half the places in town sold for less.

The properties may not always be in the neighborhoods you most prefer and they may need more work than you might like. But as long as a building is livable (or can be made so quickly) and a neighborhood is passable, then you can get started building your real-estate empire.

GETTING FOCUSED

And the beginning actually starts well before you're ready to buy a property.

You will need to decide early on what kind of properties you want to specialize in. What's your market niche? What kind of real-estate empire do you see for yourself in 10 years? Owning one or two houses or small apartment buildings that you rent out to supplement your salary?

WHERE THE MONEY IS

Here are a few money sources you can explore.

Banks and mortgage companies. Usually, you can borrow for smaller properties (buildings under five units) through the residential-lending departments of most banks or mortgage companies. If you also plan to live in the property, you will likely qualify for very high loan-to-value ratios (loans of 90 percent, or even more, of the purchase price) and interest rates will be lower. Larger buildings and other commercial properties are handled through "commercial lending" departments. The bankers will pore over your deal, making sure that the building will cover the loan costs and that they will get their payments (first, of course). Expect to borrow no more than 75 percent of the price or the appraised value, whichever is lower. On the plus side, if you have found a good property at a good price, the banker will demonstrate considerable flexibility and help in innumerable ways to see that the deal gets done.

Partners. Fifty percent of something is better than 100 percent of nothing. So which would you rather have—full ownership of a property that loses $200 a month or half ownership of one that makes $200? You can structure your partnership any way you wish. Obviously, if both of you put up equal amounts of money and equally participate in managing the property, you will both be entitled to 50 percent of the income and the appreciation. More likely, however, is a partnership in which you do most of the work and your partner puts up most of the money. In that case, you will need to see that the partner receives some ongoing as well as long-term benefits.

Friends and family. Just some cautionary comments here. You can't choose your family, but, fortunately, you can choose whom you do your business with. An "Uncle Al" interest rate inevitably comes with Uncle Al's interest in your business. Be sure that your relationship can weather the added strain of doing business together. And keep it strictly business. The IRS frowns on sweetheart family deals that don't conform to standard business practices, so avoid "no-interest" loans or loans that aren't paid back.

Private or "hard-money" lenders. At best, private lenders can make deals happen when no one else can. At worst they are Tony Sopranos. It is often much easier to borrow money on real estate than on other business ventures. Money people who might not give you the time of day if you are trying to open a new gourmet coffee bar will gladly hear what you have to say if you are buying an income-producing apartment building. These loans are usually approved within days and are often funded in two weeks or less. But the costs will be quite high. Interest rates in the teens are not uncommon, and the lender may require 5 percent to 10 percent in up-front "discount" points. If you are still not discouraged, you can find private lenders through real-estate brokers, lawyers, escrow agents and title-company officers. They even advertise in the "money-to-lend" listings in the classifieds.

Sellers. Yes, sometimes the seller will help you do the buying. It's quite common to have a seller "take back" 5 percent or 10 percent of the purchase price and carry it as a second mortgage for a few years. You can expect fairly low borrowing costs and few hassles since the seller is intimately familiar with the property. One big drawback, however, is that the seller likely will insist on a higher price if he agrees to lend you money. Investing truism: "His price, your terms; your price, his terms."

❦

Or do you see yourself working full-time as a landlord and property investor, maybe owning a few hundred apartments? Maybe you aren't into apartments at all, and want to own shopping centers or office buildings, or even become a developer who transforms farmland into a modern edge city.

This is a business you are making, and you need to start with a well-defined vision of that business.

And once you determine your focus, you will need to learn as much as you can about that business as it functions in your area. Just as all real estate is local, all real-estate practices are local as well. Yes, there are universal ways business is done, but there are local peculiarities that you need to know about. In Chicago, for instance, landlords traditionally write leases so that they end on the same day all over the city (try booking a moving van!). In Dallas, landlords have been known to require the payment of "nonrefundable" security deposits from new tenants.

We'll go into more detail in chapters 6 and 7 about what types of buildings and what to look for. We'll stick to general concepts here.

So what do you look for? And how do you know it when you find it?

You start by scanning the Internet and newspaper classifieds and driving around some neighborhoods. And here, for a moment, you can think a bit like a homeowner: You want the best neighborhood and the best building in it that you can afford. It's OK to be subjective here. We'll show you how to evaluate buildings financially in the next chapter.

For now, determine some subjective equation that works for you, one that takes into account the neighborhood, the building, the price, income and potential. They all must work together for you because there are plenty of variables that can't be quantified. Do you like the building's architecture? Is the neighborhood someplace you want to walk in at night with a month's rent (in cash) in your pocket? Do the kind of people you want to do business with live here or want to live here? Is the building the kind of place you want to own?

GETTING HELP AND BUILDING A NETWORK

You need to develop a network of real-estate professionals. Among the people you will need are a lender, a broker, a lawyer, an accountant and a contractor, whose services you can call upon as needed. We will encounter other network candidates through the book, but consider this your core group. Make these contacts before you go shopping as you will want to move quickly when a good deal appears.

Marc Asselin and his partners (his brother-in-law and his father-in-law) trade in properties in the Boynton Beach, Florida, area. They concentrate on buying and selling vacant lots that they can buy for a fraction of their developed value, and hold on to them until a buyer comes along. Mr. Asselin has even developed his own "investor network" that puts potential land buyers in touch with other landowners.

"You'd be surprised how many of the people you know are involved in real estate, if you ask them," he says. Mr. Asselin, a software engineer, built his network starting with just the real-estate agent who sold him his home. Then the network expanded to include an attorney and an accountant. "My attorney was a friend, and he just happened to specialize in real estate," says Mr. Asselin. "And my accountant is actually a corporate accountant who walked us through the tax implications of limited liability companies, S corporations and all the other ways of setting up."

The important thing in building your network of contacts and associates is you find people who are realistic and know their local real-estate market. You're looking for people who can help you acquire properties because you are unlikely to find the best—and best-priced—places just scanning newspaper or Web listings all alone.

You need contacts in the real-estate world. You need people who know properties that are coming on the market and who will alert you to them. You need people who can help you get your mortgage money and close a deal quickly. And you need people who can help you take over and start managing your new property.

As Mr. Asselin learned, there are more people out there to help you get going in real estate than you might guess. And you can always find more. For one thing, you can meet people in real-estate class.

While certainly not required of real-estate investors, a real-estate license doesn't hurt. It helps to establish you as a professional, which has distinct tax advantages, and it lets you negotiate as a professional, which can result in sales-commission savings for you. Getting a license is a fairly short classroom effort—45 hours in New York State to get a salesperson's license, 63 hours in Florida—and an easy test.

YOUR TEAM

Your **lender** is the most important person you need to know because, other than your spouse or an actual business partner, your lender will be the closest person to you. As the primary source of funds, he or she will be the person most responsible for getting you and keeping you in the real-estate business. Interview potential lenders early. Tell them what you want to do and show them your financial ability and sincerity. Find out what they are looking for in the deals they make and what kind of business plan they are going to want to see from you. No lender will OK a loan without reviewing a property's finances or the property itself, but you can and should get the process rolling by having your personal portions of the loan application (tax returns, employment information, etc.) in the works well ahead of finding a property. Going into your negotiations for a property, you want the self-assurance that you and your deal will qualify for a loan. Indeed, having your finances already lined up could be a powerful negotiating tool that could help you shave some of the asking price.

Many real-estate schemers suggest avoiding **real-estate agents.** But why? If your goal is to acquire reasonably priced investment properties, why shut yourself off from a potentially valuable source of information? Real-estate agents often know of available properties long before they actually go on the market, and they certainly maintain their own networks of potential buyers and sellers. If you have relationships with a number of agents, all of whom know you are a serious buyer, you will be as valuable to them as they are to you because they will be able to tell sellers they have a buyer ready to deal.

Even in states such as California where you don't need a **lawyer** to handle a real-estate transaction, as an investor and property owner, you are going to need the services of an attorney to write and review sales contracts and leases. If you are planning to own and operate your income properties under any kind of partnership or corporate arrangement, you will need a lawyer to help you set those up and file the appropriate documents with your state. You will also want an attorney who can help you with tenant-landlord issues that will come up.

As you will see in chapter 5, your **accountant** can be a big moneymaker for you. Real-estate-related tax laws are constantly changing. An accountant who can save you a couple of thousand dollars a year in taxes is well worth the expense.

Like any homeowner, a new property investor is going to have to learn to do a lot of basic repair and upkeep—it doesn't take many visits from a plumber to eat up a month's profit. But you will still need a trusted **contractor** to evaluate buildings and to do the really big jobs, such as replacing a roof or installing energy-efficient windows. Better to use a contractor than a property inspector (here come the protests from the inspection crowd!) when you look over a new place. Inspectors are valuable; a good one who finds a cracked foundation or some other high-cost problem can save you from a bad deal or thousands of dollars of extra expenses. But an inspector will point out problems but is unlikely to tell you what has to be fixed right away and what can slide for a bit; nor is the inspector likely to be able to come up with a better cost estimate than the contractor. That will be especially valuable when you make your offer on the building.

※

Melbourne, Florida, investor Carl Andren, who has built an extensive online network of real-estate contacts, decided to go for his agent's license after he began trading in single-family homes. He took the real-estate license plunge for two reasons, he says: first, to trim the 3 percent commission that went to the agent who represented him, and second, to gain full access to the local Multiple Listing Service, the real-estate industry's proprietary databank of properties for sale.

Real-estate class is also a place where you can find a mentor—someone like Hal Wilson, a real-estate agent and entrepreneur who has helped to educate two generations of Nashville area real-estate professionals and investors. He started teaching real-estate prelicensing classes at a local college before going into the real-estate business full-time in the 1980s. He estimates that he has bought and sold 500 houses over the last 20 years. Today, he has a weekly real-estate radio show and owns a full-service brokerage, a house rehabbing business and more than 80 residential rental properties.

Mr. Wilson is widely credited as one of the creators of Sylvan Woods, now one of Nashville's most desirable inner-city neighborhoods. Mr. Wilson and other urban pioneers created Sylvan Woods out of a down-at-the-heels no-name backwater of run-down houses. He started buying properties for just a few thousand dollars and rehabbing them, some for rental income and others to sell. Today, renovated Sylvan Woods houses regularly sell for well over $200,000, and top neighborhood prices are in the half-million-dollar range.

He calls his own investing philosophy "driving for dollars," searching for derelict, abandoned or otherwise below-average diamonds-in-the-rough houses and buildings in neighborhoods that are showing improvement.

It's a way of doing business that he has taught to hundreds of local landlords and investors through his classes, his personal appearances, his radio show and through the 500-member Real Estate Investors of Nashville network (http://www.reintn.net). The group, which meets once a month or so, gives local landlords a place to get to know each other and to swap stories while making contacts with lenders, contractors and other real-estate professionals. A recent speaker at one of the club's monthly gatherings was one of the people running the local government's building department—just the kind of person who can make or break a small landlord's or property rehabber's business.

Most cities have similar organizations. Ask around. The Internet is also a good source. Yahoo! lists more than 5,000 local, national and international real-estate investing groups (http://finance.dir.groups.yahoo.com/dir/Business_Finance/Real_Estate). And a bit further up the investing ladder are pay sites such as the Creative Investors network (http://www.thecreativeinvestor.com).

To find investors' groups in your area, go to http:// www.reiclub.com or just try Googling (example: "real estate" investor Chicago).

There is a lot of buying and selling and forging of ad hoc partnerships that go on in these kinds of groups, especially at the local level. Most important, this group can help you find properties to buy.

Look around. Be skeptical. Listen to your inner bull detector. Avoid schemers. Avoid real-estate investing gurus and other blowhards who make money selling investment seminars or "get-rich-quick-and-easy" real-estate books. These guys make their money feeding fantasies.

As the nation's real-estate frenzy reached a full boil in 2005, the real-estate schemers went into hyperdrive. Nowhere was this more evident than in a series of Real Estate Wealth Expos in Los Angeles, New York and other big cities. Thousands of would-be Donald Trumps came to hear, well, Donald Trump and other marquee princes of the rich-and-fabulous lifestyles, extol the virtues of real-estate investing to huge pep-rally-type assemblies. The crowds were worked into fever pitches by the likes of motivational guru Anthony Robbins and *Rich Dad, Poor Dad* maven Robert Kiyosaki. They appeared like rock stars, live on stage in giant arenas and on huge TV screens.

Organizers of the Expos claimed 50,000 attendees paid up to $250 each for a weekend of speeches, seminars and exhibits. Exhibitors hawked "investment" condos in Las Vegas, Miami, Panama, the Dominican Republic—even in such off-the-beaten-path spots as Dubai and Bulgaria. "Wealth through property!" declared one booth's banner. "Become a millionaire in three years or less," promised another.

Among the featured speakers were not only the lineup of late-late-night TV household names, but dozens of other lesser-known real-estate professionals who have made themselves rich by selling investing plans.

Their messages? You can get rich investing in (pick one)

tax liens, foreclosures, commercial properties, abandoned properties, discounted mortgages, auctions, land, you name it by making use of a "secret" investing formula for wealth.

Can you? Well, yes, sure, some people can and do. You can get rich at lots of things. Are you likely to? Not really.

Yes, the gurus trot out testimonials from one or two people who followed the plan and reaped their big rewards. (One guru offers seminar discounts to students who let him cite their success stories.) But the gurus never talk about the hundreds of people who shelled out thousands of dollars for investing programs but never got past the first tape in the "secrets-to-wealth" plan or the first chapter of the "real-estate-riches" workbook.

At the Expo in New York, the host of a commercial property seminar offered his $10,000 package of home-study materials for the special "show price" of just $1,500. Before the guru had even wrapped up his spiel, eager audience members had rushed the sales clerks at the back table.

Any one of them could have learned a lot more driving around for a day with someone like Jack Friedman, a philosopher-musician-landlord in Nashville. He'll take you around to his properties in his '99 Ford Escort with all his tools—wrenches, pliers, hammers, whatever it takes—in the backseat.

And Mr. Friedman will tell you what 20 years of investing has taught him, all for the price of the barbecue platter at Corky's.

"I am in most ways an anomaly," he avers. "I borrowed relatively little. I didn't leverage anything; I didn't use anybody else's money. I was lucky enough to find a few below-market buys, and I do 95 percent of my own work. In short, I've never done one of the sexy ways people envision doing real estate."

Like most of the people you will meet in this book, Mr. Friedman *is* the classic millionaire next door—that famously frugal, unassuming, invisible, yet quite well-to-do American who bears none of the vulgar, clichéd trappings of wealth displayed in TV infomercials. There's no McMansion with a Mer-

NEWBIE, BEWARE

John T. Reed, an iconoclastic California writer and real-estate newsletter publisher and writer of frank, down-to-earth advice books, has posted on his Web site (http://www.johntreed.com) a list of what to avoid in a real-estate investing guru. I can't improve on it. Among his 44 tip-offs:

- They emphasize a luxurious lifestyle showing how they and their successful students live extravagantly with "executive jets, limos, yachts, mansions, five-star hotels, exotic resorts, or expensive cars."

- They stress motivational material. "It is dishonest to promise how-to information, then deliver a bunch of 'you-can-do-it' platitudes instead."

- They claim to do a lot of deals, when "there aren't enough hours in a day" to run their guru businesses alongside a real-estate business.

- They push "no-down, low-down" buying strategies. "The typical real-estate millionaire did not get where he is by using nothing-down, lease-option (for acquisitions), or partner techniques. But the typical real-estate guru did get where he is by persuading low-net-worth individuals to believe that they can get rich making no-cash-down, real-estate acquisitions."

For a more comprehensive, and varied, look at a large number of real-estate gurus, visit http://www.realestatecoursereviews.com, where individuals file Amazon-like reviews of various seminars and programs.

cedes in the driveway, no $1,000 suits, no Rolex watch, no yacht, no corporate jet, no private Caribbean island.

What Mr. Friedman does have, however, are an enviable net worth, no significant debts (not even mortgages), a steady income that lets him live where and as he wants, a secure retirement and no money worries. He has, in short, the "financial freedom" that is so elusive to so many Americans and leads thousands of them to seek the misguidance of the get-rich-quick gurus.

"I'm blessed," he says, "to be completely satisfied with a very modest standard of living."

How many people are "completely satisfied" with their financial lives?

You could do worse learning from someone like that as you try to step into the real-estate business.

CHAPTER 3

THE THREE QUESTIONS

No man acquires property without acquiring with it a little arithmetic.

— RALPH WALDO EMERSON

Once you have figured out where your starting capital will come from and focused on the type of buildings you want to own and enlisted the aid of your network, you will need to start looking at specific properties. In this and the next chapter, we will look at how you evaluate properties and buy them.

But first things first: Any real-estate investor—whether considering a single-family home, an apartment building, a shopping center or a giant office complex—must ask some basic questions about the property.

You should buy an investment property with no more emotion than you would have investing in a stock, a bond or anything else. It's only business. So always ask three questions:

- **"Is buying this property the best use of my money?"**

- **"Will this property pay for itself?"**

- **"Can I increase the value of this property?"**

If you can't answer yes to each question, don't buy the place.

And how you go about answering those questions is the fundamental issue of all investing. It's what Wall Street investment bankers call "due diligence," the period of intense study that precedes a merger, acquisition or other deal. You, too, need to do your due diligence before you buy a building. Let's see how.

"IS BUYING THIS PROPERTY THE BEST USE OF MY MONEY?"

Increasingly, experienced landlords and investors are pulling back on their property buying as building prices in many boom regions have gotten too high to produce adequate income. By early 2006, Carl Andren, the Melbourne, Florida, investor, had reduced his holdings to just 3 rental houses—down from his peak of 11 properties. For a man who 10 years ago was buying foreclosed three-bedroom, two-bath houses for just $1,000 each, plus closing costs, the current going rate for his preferred type of investment property—$130,000 to $150,000—is just too rich.

As a property buyer, Mr. Andren has been effectively priced out of his own market. He doesn't expect houses to continue increasing in value at the same sizzling rates, and, for now, it's too hard for him to find undervalued properties. And rents are not high enough to justify paying higher prices. So he's selling.

Mr. Friedman in Nashville is in much the same boat. He, too, has been unable to find under-market properties, so he has been diversifying his investments. Lately, he's been exploring the moneylending side of the real-estate business.

Experienced property investors know when to bow out or

cash out because there is a simple, readily accessible number that tells anyone whether any piece of real estate—or for that matter, any investment—is worth putting money into: the current interest rate on a 10-year Treasury note. Think of it as the national "internal rate of return" (IRR), a financial formulation that investors use to determine the practicality of a particular investment. IRR answers the question "Is this a better use of my money than doing with it what I'm already doing?"

For as long as the government continues to pay its creditors, there will be no safer investment you can make than to lend the United States money. With absolute certainty, you can count on being paid your interest on time and getting your principal back. So you must consider the current Treasury yield as the bare minimum you should make on your investment. (It's now about 5 percent a year and rising—up from where it was just two years ago but still way, way down from the real-estate-investment-killing rate of 16 percent in 1981.) And since anyone can make 5 percent simply by loaning money to the government, anything lower than the Treasury rate is a bad deal and doesn't compensate you for your risk.

On a scale of risk versus reward, Treasurys are just about perfect—zero risk, guaranteed reward. Treasurys will usually pay more than bank savings accounts or short-term certificates of deposit, more than most stock dividends and less than most other bonds or loans. At the riskier end of the scale might be newly issued stock in a start-up technology company that pays no dividend but might be the next Microsoft or Google. Your $10,000 could be worth $10 million in 10 years. Or the company could go bankrupt and you'd lose your entire investment, as millions of investors did when they bought stock in 1990s Internet companies like Pets.com and Webvan.

Think of most real-estate investments in the midrange of the scale, nicely rewarding but not so risky that you will lose all your money if something goes wrong. It's not easy to lose money in real estate, especially after you have done several deals, but it can be done. And if an investor can make 5 percent on his or her money risk free, why buy into a real-estate market in which rents can't cover operating costs and values over the next few years are likely to remain—at best—stagnant or perhaps decline?

Treasurys are a good investor's benchmark, then, because they give you a floor to judge value. So let's rephrase the original question a bit: "Is this property going to make more money than a Treasury bond?"

Traditionally, we certainly expect so. That's because one of the most touted advantages of real-estate investing is high "leverage," the difference between the price of a piece of property and what you actually pay for it. Leverage lets you acquire properties for far less than they actually cost. Think of it this way: A typical property buyer pays just $1 and borrows $4.

If you have ever bought a house, you know the routine. For decades, the traditional standard was that you put 20 percent down on a house and a bank lent you 80 percent. But the old standards have gone by the wayside. First came 10 percent down loans, then 5 percent or less. Today, it's possible, though risky, to buy fixer-upper properties with no money down and mortgage-rehab loans covering 125 percent of the property's price. (Such loans are risky because in a stagnant or falling market, you may not be able to increase the value of the house enough to cover the mortgage debt. Indeed, a highly leveraged property owner could find himself "upside down," owing more than the house is worth.)

For investors, leverage is a good thing. But for homeowners, its benefits can be greatly exaggerated. Real-estate hucksters, who often oversell the concept of homes as investments, usually overstate the value of leverage to home buyers. Leverage does allow homeowners to buy much-bigger, more-expensive houses than they might otherwise. But that's not necessarily a good thing.

Remember: Homes aren't investment properties. That's

mainly because the interest you pay on the mortgage eats up so much of the appreciation. Do the math: If you buy a $300,000 house with a 95 percent loan at 6 percent, and the house appreciates at 5 percent annually, you're just treading water. Sure, you can do well when prices are going up 15 percent or 20 percent a year, but those are unsustainable rates over the long term—like Internet stocks in 1999.

But for smart real-estate investors, leverage is very good. If you have a property that pays for itself—that is, if other people cover its operating expenses and its debt service by paying you rent—then leverage indeed works wonders for your investment returns.

Real-estate investing is all about "cash flow"—a term that applies to all business enterprises but has as many meanings as there are investment books. Indeed, at *The Wall Street Journal,* our writers are instructed to explain cash flow in myriad ways, depending on the industry they are writing about.

Generally, real-estate professionals define cash flow as the money that remains after paying the operating expenses and the mortgage of income-producing real estate.

When you ask if buying a building is the best use of your money, you are also asking whether it will produce sufficient cash flow. Your job as an owner and manager of income property is to generate cash by maximizing your property's income and minimizing your property's expenses. The more cash you have to work with, the more you can invest in your business to expand it, improve your profit margins, pay off your mortgage debts, raise your income and increase your wealth. If you do not manage your cash effectively, you will fail.

Here is one year's cash-flow analysis for a $400,000, four-unit apartment building in Houston. The place has a $300,000 mortgage at 6 percent. Each apartment rents for $800 a month. Much of what's in this and the next chapter will decipher what each of these line items means.

For now, just look at the top line and the bottom line. The

NOTHING DOWN!

There's leverage, and then there's *leverage*.

To listen to infomercial schemers, the Holy Grail of real-estate investing is a "zero-down" deal on a property that you buy for next to nothing and then turn around and sell quickly for full market value. Now that's a return on your investment! And, unfortunately, for most of us, it's a deal that is just too good to be true.

It would be wrong to call such hyperhawked schemes scams, but for most people they simply won't work. The pool of properties is too small, and the body of competitors is far too large. Still, such deals can be done.

While there are plenty of variations, depending on the TV guru, the "no-money-down" deals generally work in very similar ways. Here's the basic run-down.

Find a distressed property. These are usually fixer-upper houses whose owners have fallen behind in their payments. Gurus often suggest driving through neighborhoods and looking for properties that are not being maintained. You can also check public foreclosure lists along with death, bankruptcy or divorce notices. More advanced dealers in distressed properties rely on a network of "bird dogs,"—who can be other investors or real-estate agents, lenders and lawyers—to help them find prospects.

Make an offer. Knock on the door or otherwise contact the owners. Confirm their situation and tell them you can save their credit rating by taking over their payments. In some of these deals, you act as a middleman, taking just a modest finder's fee from an investor. You can also play the game yourself by offering the delinquent homeowner a "subject-to" sales contract in which you take over ownership of the house and pay the mortgage holder what's due, usually just a few thousand dollars. Another variation: Contact the lender directly and make a lowball offer on a soon-to-be foreclosed property. In any case, you need to buy the place well below its repaired value—30 percent to 40 percent below market.

Fix it up. These kinds of properties usually require a lot of yard work and cosmetic repairs since homeowners stop maintaining their properties months before they stop making mortgage payments. Keep your improvements and your costs to a minimum. Just do what you have to do to put the place up for sale—Formica countertops, not granite; tile bathrooms, not marble. Get the work done as quickly as possible, and get the place on the market.

Sell it. Since your costs are, presumably, low, you should be able to put a very attractive price on the newly rehabbed house. Close the deal and pocket your profits, which, if you pulled the entire deal together in less than a year, will be taxed as regular income, not at the lower capital-gains rate.

※

property's rental income covers all its operating expenses and mortgage payments and, after taxes, puts about $5,750 in the owner's pocket. That's cash flow.

Now let's say that John, a young oil-company manager, wants to buy this building.

He already knows the building produces an annual before-tax cash flow of $5,000. But that's just 1.25 percent a year! That's way, way below the Treasury bond rate. Why in the world would John want the hassles of managing a building for such a measly payback?

The reason is *leverage*. To buy that $400,000 building, John will spend just $100,000 and borrow the rest. But that 25 percent

IT'S ALL ABOUT CASH FLOW	
Rental Income	**$38,400**
Vacancy loss (15%)	($5,760)
Operating expenses	($6,000)
Net operating income	$26,640
Mortgage interest	($17,900)
Depreciation	($10,847)
Taxable income	($2,107)
Net operating income	$26,640
Annual debt service (principal & interest)	($21,584)
Pretax cash flow	$5,056
Tax savings @ 33%	$695
After-Tax Cash Flow	**$5,751**

"BEST USE OF MY MONEY?"	
Sale Price	$550,000
Loan balance	($279,163)
Sale transaction costs	($55,000)
Down payment	($100,000)
Pretax Profit	**$115,837**
Capital-gain tax	($10,909)
Depreciation-recapture tax	($14,250)
After-Tax Profit	**$90,678**
Return on investment (ROI)	91%
Internal rate of return (IRR)	19%

of the purchase price buys him 100 percent of the property. And more important from an investor's point of view, it buys him 100 percent of the $5,000 a year income. Because John will have acquired a $400,000 property for just $100,000, that measly 1.25 percent return is now a much more attractive annual yield of 5 percent.

And it gets better. Over time, John will be able to raise rents gradually and increase the value of the building. With just modest rent increases, John's before-tax cash flow could reach $8,400 by the end of his fifth year of ownership.

And it will get even better when John decides to sell the building. Let's say that after five years of ownership, John decides it's time to trade up to a larger property. He sets a price at $550,000. Like a homeowner, his $100,000 has bought him 100 percent of the appreciation. But unlike a homeowner, John has not paid any of the costs of borrowing money or maintaining the property; his tenants did that for him. So rather than treading water or losing money on the deal, John will have quite successfully invested his money and made a handsome $90,000 profit.

Well, 19 percent a year sure beats a 5 percent Treasury yield, so this deal definitely fits the bill. John's total return far surpasses what he could make in government bonds. And while he may not have hit on the next Microsoft, he's not going to be left holding worthless stock certificates, either. (By the way, you'll see in chapter 5 how the tax laws will actually help John increase his return well beyond this.)

Next question . . .

"WILL THIS PROPERTY PAY FOR ITSELF?"

Real investments don't cost you more money every month. They are supposed to make money for you, not take it away from you.

"I'm a very conservative investor," says Mr. Andren. "A property has to pay for itself. Breakeven is OK. Negative? Never."

Think about it. Would you spend $10,000 to buy 100 shares of stock and then pay an extra $100 a month just to hold on to the shares? Of course not. But far too many novice real-estate investors do just that. They go into deals that can't pay for themselves, deciding they will cover the monthly loss or "negative" out of their salaried income. The doomed investor tells himself that he can carry the negative on the property for a while, until he can raise rents or sell the place at a profit. This is a formula for failure.

Let's go back to John in Houston and change some of the building's numbers a bit, cutting the monthly rent on each of the four apartments to $600 from $800, thus reducing the building's overall income to $28,800 from $38,400. John still thinks the building is a good buy at $400,000. He's crunched the numbers and knows he can cover the monthly shortfall from his oil-company salary, and he's seen and read that real-estate prices have been going up 15 percent a year for the past three years. He figures that if values rise at just half of what they have been, he'll be able to sell the place for $550,000 in five years.

John's making a dangerous wager, and it's one that this house is certain to lose.

"NEGATIVES" DON'T PAY	
Rental Income	**$28,800**
Vacancy loss (15%)	($4,320)
Operating expenses	($6,000)
Net operating income	$18,480
Mortgage interest	($17,900)
Depreciation	($10,847)
Taxable income	($10,267)
Net operating income	$18,480
Annual debt service (principal & interest)	($21,584)
Pretax cash flow	($3,104)
Tax savings @ 33%	$3,388
After-Tax Cash Flow	**$284**

Novice real-estate investors such as John should always base their purchases on the actual income that a building brings in, not on what they think they can get in the future or what a building will be worth years from now. John is paying way too much for the income he's receiving. He's also unlikely to be able to sell the building for what he hopes five years out.

Now to be fair, John is technically breaking even here. He's using tax loopholes available to real-estate investors to compensate for the building's failure to pay for itself. If he's lucky, he might be able to ride this out for a while until he can raise his rents enough to cover his costs.

If he's like the rest of us, however, he's probably facing a disaster.

John's expenses will rise, too. Property taxes will go up. Tenants will skip out. The roof will have to be replaced. Pipes will break. Carpets will get ruined. John's building should be paying for these kinds of predictable problems. But if he is shelling out more money every month than the building is bringing in, he will end up covering the additional costs himself—tax breaks or no tax breaks. If he wants to upgrade the building, he'll have to pay for the improvements himself. In short, John will just dig himself deeper and deeper into the hole with each month's new crisis or problem.

WHY "NEGATIVES" ARE BAD	
Sale Price	$425,000
Loan balance	($279,163)
Sale transaction costs	($42,500)
Down payment	($100,000)
Pretax Profit	$3,337
Capital-gain tax	$0
Depreciation-recapture tax	($6,534)
After-Tax Profit (Loss)	($3,197)
Return on investment (ROI)	−3.2%
Internal rate of return (IRR)	−0.46%

Then, piling insult on injury, John's building will end up less valuable to a buyer because it doesn't make enough money. Think about it: John's paying $21,000 a year to lose $3,000. Who's going to make a deal like that? Not a reader of this book. You'll see shortly how to value properties. But for now, you should know that John's building will probably be worth no more than about $425,000 when he sells it in five years. So here are his dismal results: a loss of $3,000.

John should have stayed with Treasury bonds.

As we will see in chapter 5, the phantom "paper" losses associated with real-estate depreciation are great; the government pays for those. But real losses? No, thanks. That comes out of your pocket and takes away from your long-term returns.

So if you want to make a deal, you must structure your purchase so that the building covers its costs. And you have every right during negotiations to question the seller on every dollar that goes in and out of the building.

Individual houses and small apartment buildings may not have very useful records; the landlord may not have much more information than bank statements showing regular rental payments and regular mortgage payments and other expenses. But owners of larger buildings should have much more professional bookkeeping. And if they don't, be wary.

WHEN NEGATIVES CAN WORK

It's possible to make negative cash flows work, but you need more than one property to pull it off. So first-time investors should steer clear.

Understand that like any other kind of investor, at any particular point in time you are going to have individual holdings that perform better than others, some that make money and some that don't. That's the essence of any kind of diversified investment portfolio.

The trick is determining whether your loser building has the potential to become a winner. That is largely a function of what the current rents are and whether they can be raised substantially in an acceptable length of time. You will never get Beverly Hills rents in South Central Los Angeles.

It is perfectly all right, and a reasonable business practice, to have one property temporarily cover the costs of another—to use the income from building A, for example, to cover a negative at building B as you renovate or prepare it for a general rent increase.

The more diversified your real-estate portfolio, the more you can handle negative cash flows. If, for example, you are convinced that a run-down warehouse district is going to become your city's new chic loft neighborhood, you may need to buy some properties long before they can pay for themselves.

Again, it all depends on whether you have other profitable properties that can offset the negative cash flows.

Mr. Andren tells a story about his first effort at buying a small hotel on his beach town's main drag a couple of blocks from the Atlantic Ocean. It was a bit down at the heels, but Mr. Andren and his partners liked its location and saw considerable potential for it. They agreed to pay $550,000, based on the existing owner's claim of $130,000 income and $60,000 profit. Then they asked to see the books.

LOOK AT THE LEASES

Leases are what make a piece of real estate an investment. They are the contracts that outline how much money a property makes and, ultimately, what a property is worth. A building makes no money unless people pay to live in it or operate their businesses from it. As the saying goes, an oral lease isn't worth the paper it's printed on. Get it in writing. Leases protect landlords and tenants.

We'll discuss leases more in chapter 7, when we look at commercial properties. For now, know that residential and commercial leases are really quite different animals. Residential leases are fairly straightforward, and owners of small buildings can usually get along with the lease forms that can be bought at stationery stores or downloaded from the Web. You'll want to make some modifications, but the general terms are pretty standard.

❧

"Our books are really for taxes," explained the owner, as he revealed that the hotel was not making a profit at all. Instead, it was losing $50,000 a year.

"I can't take this to a bank!" Mr. Andren bellowed.

After inspecting the building's records, Mr. Andren and his partners went back to their calculators and put together a new offer of $415,000.

The old owner held firm, and Mr. Andren and his partners walked away. He reports that the owner has not been able to unload the hotel since and that the building is now in much worse shape.

There's a lesson here: There is no shame in not buying.

As part of the due-diligence process, you should inspect the seller's books. This is usually done after you make an initial offer—contingent on a full inspection of the property itself and reviewing the building's accounts—but before a final contract is signed. You should expect to see a proper accounting of all the building's income and expenses, and copies of bills and checks, along with copies of all leases and proof that the tenants' security and other deposits are in a separate bank account or otherwise properly accounted for and set aside. This is also the period when you will have your contractor inspect the property, looking for structural problems that could affect the value of the property.

Think of this as the equivalent of having a mechanic inspect a used car. If it turns out that something is wrong, you are not likely to pay what you initially offered.

You are not bound to the price you initially agreed upon. You and the seller are just engaged at this point: No one has said, "I do." But once you are this far along in the process, the seller is usually as committed as you are, so you can make reasonable adjustments to your offer after you learn more about the property. You are unlikely to make the kind of adjustment that Mr. Andren sought. So like the song says, know when to walk away.

Be resolute. Don't be a jerk, but recognize that your opening offer was just that—an opening. It is only after you have had a chance to thoroughly inspect the building and the rental business that you can set an informed price for the property. If that $400,000 four-unit apartment building needs an additional $50,000 of repairs before you can start making money, it will not be nearly as attractive as one that's in top condition. A $500,000 building that's in good shape could, in the long run, end up a better deal for you.

So after you know the true costs of buying and operating the building, play hardball. Revise your offer to reflect what you learn. Be realistic, and stick to what you now know the building is worth to you. And always be prepared to give up on the deal.

In some cases, getting the deal done may mean you will need to put more money down, or you may need to bring in a partner who will put up more cash to cover repairs. Perhaps you can significantly cut some of the building's expenses by doing work yourself or finding someone who will do it cheaper.

Property owner Alex Levin says the difference between his properties in the Buffalo, New York, area just breaking even and making a profit is that his father does much of the maintenance. That's especially good for Mr. Levin, since he lives on the other side of the world. Although he's from Buffalo and his family lives there, Mr. Levin works and lives in Moscow. He visits home once or twice a year—that's when he buys his properties—but he leaves the basic day-to-day maintenance and rent collecting for his 11 buildings to his father and mother.

Landlords can cut their expenses. Or they can come up with ways to increase revenues. One thing you want to be careful about doing, however, is quickly raising rents on the existing tenants. First, you might not be able to. You are bound by the terms of any existing leases when you take over a building. But beyond that, quickly raising rents is a good way to alienate your new customers. What kind of impression would you, the new landlord, be making on your customers if the first thing you do when you take over ownership of their building is raise their rents?

Yes, you want to raise the rents. And yes, you know that part of the reason the building is an attractive deal is because the income is not up to its potential. But recognize that there are any number of perfectly good reasons why the rents are what they are. The previous owner may have had little or no debt, in which case he wasn't under any financial pressure to raise rents. The building may need updating. Or it may have longtime tenants, whom the previous owner valued for stability over marginal income increases. *Worst case:* The building could be under some kind of legal rent control that sets rents artificially low.

You should have a good reason to raise rents beyond the marginal yearly increases that are planned and laid out in the leases. You should improve the building or offer new services if you want to increase your rental income significantly. Remember: What to you is a property is to your tenants a home. It's bad management and unneighborly to structure your deal so that the only way you can pay for your building is to burden the people who live in it by charging them more for the same level of service that they got before you arrived.

If you do, your tenants will not take good care of the property, will be demanding about repairs and will move as soon as they can find a better deal—forcing you to spend money on searching for new renters. And beyond all that, it is simply heartless and cruel to arbitrarily charge people more to live in their homes simply because you can.

"CAN I INCREASE THE VALUE OF THIS PROPERTY?"

The answer to this question may seem obvious—real estate always goes up, right? But it is, in fact, far from a certainty. Real-estate prices tanked in large parts of Texas in the mid-1980s when oil prices collapsed, and in many parts of the state they are only now recovering. In Southern California, where generations thought rising real-estate prices were written into the Bill of Rights, defense industries shuttered with the end of the Cold War, sending housing prices into a tailspin that they didn't pull out of for a decade. Real-estate prices are affected by the local employment rates as much as they are by interest rates.

Good idea: Before you buy, check out what's going on with the big local employers. Layoffs on the way? Plant closings? The real-estate market in Jackson, Mississippi, a fair-sized state capital, took a big hit in 2002 and 2003 when the collapse of WorldCom put many local renters and homeowners out of work. Especially hard hit were high-end single-family homes, bought by WorldCom employees flush with paper wealth created by their company's rapidly rising stocks. (Investors who scooped up some of those properties were doing rather well just two years later, when a new Nissan auto plant opened.)

Less suddenly, but no less devastating, has been the slow, steady decline of another medium-sized state capital, Hartford,

Connecticut. There, the local economy has been whittled away by the long death spiral of the city's longtime business engine, the insurance industry. Sale prices of residential properties lag well behind other regional metropolises such as Boston and the New York suburbs in Fairfield County, Connecticut, and commercial properties sell for less than half of what comparable buildings go for elsewhere in the Northeast.

Yes, the price of most real estate over time will increase. If you wait out temporary market shocks, maintain the property and keep it rented, you can pretty much count on it keeping up with or beating inflation over the long term. But if your property appreciates only as inflation goes up, or only as other properties around it go up, you're just running with the pack. You can do better.

"I'm not a millionaire now," says Mr. Levin, who is operating in the archetypal Old Economy region that by most criteria offers little in the way of growth or increasing property values. "But if every property I own never appreciates, I will retire a millionaire."

A real-estate investor like Mr. Levin has one big advantage over a stock investor: the ability to enhance the value of his holdings. If you own 1,000 shares of a stock, you have zero chance to improve the company's operations, increase revenues, cut costs, introduce new products or do anything else that will materially affect the performance of your shares. As a minority shareholder, your voting power is worthless. Your fate is pretty much in the hands of the managers and majority shareholders, and your stock price rides the path that the market sets.

But if you are the manager or the principal owner of an enterprise, you can make a big difference. And being a good manager—being creative, imaginative, resourceful and thrifty—can make you a lot of money.

An investment property's value is fundamentally a function of its ability to produce income. Just as the value of a stock is expressed by a "price-earnings ratio" (P/E), investment property values are expressed as "cap rates" or "rent multiples" or some other term. And unlike a home, an investment property's value transcends just size, condition, location, amenities or emotional attributes. An investment property produces income, and the landlord has the power to change that to his benefit.

From the first moment you see a property, imagine it as it could be. Be realistic. Look for opportunities that the current owner has missed. You probably won't knock down a modest 2-story, 16-unit garden-type building and replace it with a 40-story luxury condominium tower. But you can come up with amenities that you can add to the building to increase the value to the current tenants and raise their rents. Can you provide new services? Can you make more profitable use of existing spaces?

Many cable-TV or satellite companies, for instance, will make very attractive deals with landlords who sign up all the apartments in a single building. If a basic cable-TV package costs $25 to a typical apartment dweller, the owner of a 25-unit building might be able to negotiate a price of $10 or $15 for each apartment and then pass the charge on to the tenants with a $20-a-month rent increase.

Increasingly, landlords are offering wired or wireless Internet access as part of their monthly rental packages. Telephone and cable-TV companies charge $40 or more a month for Internet access, but an enterprising landlord should be able to wire a building or install a wireless network and offer profitable Internet service at a much lower cost to the tenants.

Likewise, there are space issues that can offer opportunities. In some areas, cell-phone companies rent roof space on apartment buildings for their transmitters. And most buildings have storerooms or other extra spaces that aren't used to their fullest. Is there space to put in a coin-operated laundry? Can you make more money renting out an unused garage for one tenant's second car or by dividing it and offering extra storage spaces to all the tenants? (Rule of thumb: You will make more money renting out four 25-square-foot storerooms than one 100-square-foot room.)

And what about renovations for new tenants? If you spend $10,000 upgrading a vacant $800-a-month apartment, can you get at least $42 a month more from a new tenant? That's a 5 percent annual return, which matches a Treasury note yield. How about $200? That would represent a 24 percent annual return on what it cost you to renovate, and a whopping 25 percent increase in income. However, you must coldly calculate renovations, for you don't want to end up making the apartment nicer than it can pay to be. Marble baths and stainless-steel kitchen appliances may be your preference in your own home, but will a tenant pay for them in an apartment? In chic Manhattan, maybe; in working-class Queens, not too likely.

If local laws allow "mixed use" of properties, you might try renting an apartment to a lawyer, a doctor or some other professional for use as an office. You will want your building in a location that works for an office—not on a quiet cul-de-sac, but a corner on a busy street. Office rents are usually higher than residential rents, and professionals can also be expected to pay extra for parking spaces.

The point is that the best way to increase income is to offer tenants more than they were getting before. Internet, laundry and extra storage all increase the revenues of the property and, in turn, increase the value of the property.

With these three fundamental questions in mind—"Is buying this property the best use of my money?" "Will this property pay for itself?" "Can I increase the value of this property?"—you are ready to buy a building.

CHAPTER 4

Finding, Buying and Closing the Deal

We come and go, but the land is always here. And the people who love it and understand it are the people who own it—for a little while.

— Willa Cather

The old real-estate agent's cliché—the three most important things about a single-family house are location, location, location—is just as true for an investment property. The big difference is that what's a good location for your home may not be a good location for your investment property.

Take a look around your neighborhood and town. Do you see nice single-family houses sitting next to convenience stores? Mansions sharing blocks with apartment buildings? Auto-repair shops next door to swanky boutiques?

In most places, you don't. Zoning laws and business practices tend to group like properties with like properties so that cities and towns develop with residential, commercial, industrial and other districts. You are not likely to see a residential development beside an industrial park, though you might find an outlet mall across the street from a factory.

Older cities and close-in suburbs have more "mixed-use" neighborhoods. That's where you will see older commercial areas with stores on the first floors of buildings, apartments or offices upstairs. Such districts might feature blocks of modest houses and apartments surrounding an aging factory, which today is itself far more likely to be a collection of trendy offices, shops or pricey condominiums than a manufacturing facility. In some older downtowns, you will see the upper floors of early 20th-century high-rise office buildings converted to apartments, while the lower floors have become chic restaurants, retailers or offices.

Newer cities and suburbs are far more segregated. There, you are more likely to see "strip" or automobile-oriented developments featuring wide avenues flanked by vast parking lots fronting shopping centers, big-box retailers and low-rise office buildings. Often, on side streets just behind those, you will find apartment buildings. And beyond those, single-family homes.

As that image suggests, you will find most multiunit residential properties in transitional districts, buffering single-family properties from commercial or industrial districts.

You will need to see many, many properties before you will learn what level of repair or upkeep is acceptable, what amenities are usual or what tenants are like. You are educating yourself, and no one ever learned everything he or she needed to know about an investment with one look.

So whatever you do, don't make a firm offer on the first place you see—even if it meets every criteria you think you have. You don't know enough yet to buy any place at all.

Another warning: Don't just go for cheap. You can always improve a trashy building in an up-and-coming part of town, but your property alone isn't likely to turn a trashy neighborhood into the next SoHo. It's better to be the 5th or 10th investor in a neighborhood that's already getting better than to be the first in a neighborhood that's not yet taken off.

BUY IN AREAS YOU KNOW

At the height of the real-estate boom, it was common to read stories about homeowners and real-estate professionals refinancing their expensive properties in California, the Mid-Atlantic, Florida or elsewhere and buying much cheaper properties in areas that did not see huge price run-ups.

In just five years, Californian Anthony Santana built himself a good-sized real-estate empire—and a $1 million net worth—by selling his Silicon Valley home and using its equity run-up to buy properties in the Sacramento region and, later, in other areas in the inland West.

There were plenty of success stories like Mr. Santana's throughout the real-estate boom. Investors wheeled and dealed the high appreciation of their coastal-zone homes and buildings to acquire more investment properties in other parts of the country. But as the decade wore on, there were more and more tales of efforts that went terribly wrong.

Take Australians Mark and Toni Larsen, for instance. Having enjoyed some real-estate success at home, they hooked up with some Americans who were promising 21 percent returns on quick rehabs of foreclosed houses. "Considering it's no longer possible to get 10 percent property returns in Australia," says Mr. Larsen, "the thought of a 20 percent odd return appealed."

The plan was simple: The Larsens would buy the houses; their American partners would do the quick rehabs and then sell the houses—45 days at the most. But just about everything that could go wrong did go wrong, recalls Mr. Larsen. He and his partners bought a house in upstate New York. When they took possession, the building was in much worse shape than he had been led to believe. What was going to be a quick-and-easy rehab turned out to be a much bigger job. Then there was a problem getting insurance on the place. Then his partners stopped updating him the way they had agreed.

You get the picture: It's a long, long way from New South Wales to New York. It was impossible to make the Larsens' deal work. They couldn't keep an eye on their partners or their property, and they couldn't take over the operation. At best, they were at the mercy of incompetents. At worst, con artists.

"We bought the place in May, and by October we'd had enough," says Mr. Larsen. "The Americans picked up the phone and spent two hours making excuses, but that was no good to me." Eventually, the partners agreed to buy back the house for the money that the Larsens had put up.

Even that hasn't worked out as smoothly as they had hoped. The 45-day, 20 percent return deal ended up as a nine-month interest-free loan to the Americans and a loss for the Australians, if you add up the phone calls, the registered mail and the express deliveries—even an IRS hold on the sale proceeds as the government determined whether there were any taxes due on the transaction.

In all, a big mess and a cautionary tale for novice investors. Be wary of long-distance deals. Remember, one of the attractions of real estate is you can materially affect the performance of your investments. You're not at the mercy of overindulged, overpaid CEOs or hapless boards of directors. Delegating responsibilities is fine, but abrogating them—just handing over your dough and expecting to get a fat return—is neither smart investing nor smart management.

Mr. Santana, the California investor, has mixed feelings about his long-distance operations. Yes, he's making money at them. And no, he's not had a lot of problems. But he has had some, especially with property managers who don't look in on buildings often enough or aren't available in an emergency.

"Ideally, I like to have my real-estate agents do the property managing," says, Mr. Santana. "They have an interest in the places because they're going to get the sale when we sell it. They also have a lot of contacts and are good at finding renters."

Nonetheless, novice investors should be wary of such arrangements. You can't properly manage a building from 2,000 miles away. The profit margins on single-family homes and small apartment buildings are narrow, and the farther away you are from your property, the more likely you will need to add the expense of a local manager to run the place.

Think about it: If you are in San Jose and own an apartment building in Akron, how fast can you react to a crisis? How soon will you know that a tenant has skipped out on you? How will you make sure that the snowplowing is getting done first thing after a blizzard?

Pat Trustey, a Long Island, New York, nurse and her three grown sons learned a tough lesson about absentee ownership. They bought a house in the sizzling Las Vegas market in 2005. By May, they had a tenant. By December, the tenant had stopped paying rent. A friend went over to the house. "She knocks, but nobody answers. Finally, she sees the door ajar so she just goes in. The tenant's girlfriend is sitting there. The place is atrocious. There are two dogs, two cats, and there are drugs all over the place. There are cigarette burns on the rugs."

You have to avoid those kinds of situations. While there may be ample opportunities for pure investing plays in areas far from home—a partnership, say, of New York investors who contract with a management company to operate properties in Kentucky—the need for your hands-on management is going to require that you stick to nearby areas.

And even close to home, you are going to want to concentrate your efforts. You don't want your properties situated great distances from each other so that you spend a huge chunk of your time driving from one building to another. Better to have your rental properties near your own home or office, and better to have multiple properties near each other.

"HOW DO I KNOW WHAT BUILDINGS ARE WORTH?"

Because you have looked at a lot of buildings. The real-estate agents and sellers who have shown you various properties have given you simplified financial statements for each—income statements that show what each unit pays in monthly rent, and what the owner pays for vacancies, maintenance, utilities, insurance and taxes.

Some experienced investors refer to these as "liar's statements" because they typically underreport operating expenses and inflate rents. But read skeptically, these statements should give you enough information to make an early call on a particular property. Rule of thumb: In your head, cut the income by 10 percent and increase the costs by 15 percent.

It's not your due diligence, just the first step toward making the most important calculation that any property investor makes—figuring a building's "capitalization rate."

A cap rate—the ratio between what a building costs and what it makes—is the most fundamental indicator of a property's value. It is the real-estate investor's equivalent to the stock market's "price-earnings ratio" that is used to value and compare different stocks.

Net Operating Income ÷ Purchase Price = Cap Rate

Like stock investors, landlords have all sorts of ways they crunch numbers to measure their investment performance— "gross-rent multiplier," "debt-service ratio," "return on investment" and others. But first and foremost is the relation between purchase price and net operating income, expressed as the cap rate.

Let's go back to John in Houston eyeing that $400,000, four-unit apartment building where the apartments rent for an average of $800 a month ($38,400 a year). After the owner pays all of his nonmortgage expenses, he has a net operating income left over of $26,000 a year. With just that information, John can figure the cap rate and use the result to compare the property to others he has seen. So for this case:

$26,000 ÷ $400,000 = .065 (expressed as 6.5, or 6.5%)

Translated, that means that if John were paying all cash for the building, he would see a 6.5 percent yield on his capital.

And if you've followed this far, you should be realizing how real-estate investors increase the value of their properties—the more money a building makes, the more it is worth. If $26,000 of income sells for $400,000 in a neighborhood with cap rates hovering around 6.5 percent, then $30,000 a year should be worth about $462,000. And $52,000 a year of income would be worth about $800,000.

For a buyer, a higher cap rate is best since it indicates a greater return. As a rule, similar buildings will have lower cap rates in less-risky, more-desirable neighborhoods, and higher cap rates in higher-risk, more-marginal parts of town. In a real-estate market where building incomes are rising and cap rates are declining, prices will be rising. Therefore, look for declining prices where income goes down and cap rates rise.

For the most part, neighborhood cap rates hold steady. It would be a deal almost too good to be true to find a building for sale with a cap rate in the 10 to 12 range in a neighborhood where all the other buildings are in the 6 to 8 range. (If you do, please give me a call.)

Now that John has determined the cap rate on his target property, he'll need to compare it with other income properties in the area. Real-estate agents will often quote area cap rates, but it would be wise for John to do his own calculations and to get input from others in his network of real-estate contacts.

He's already armed with income statements for a number of the places he's looked at, and he can easily compare those figures with this building's. Appraisers, other landlords and other real-estate professionals will be generally familiar with the numbers for buildings in their neighborhoods. For this example, let's say cap rates—on asking prices—in the neighborhood tend to range from 6 percent to 7 percent. John's potential buy is right in the middle.

That's a good start. But what John really wants to know are cap rates for sale prices—not what sellers asked, but what buyers paid. For those, he'll need to look at "sales comparables" that will show him what other, similar buildings in the area have sold for recently. In most states, real-estate sales figures are public records—many of which are now accessible online. At a minimum, county records should note the date of the sale, the price, the annual property tax, the overall size of the building and the number of units. Frequently, one can learn the mortgage amount as well.

John, of course, won't know the condition of the comparable buildings (unless they happen to be among those he looked at), but he will get a very good picture of what similar properties have been selling for. Many county assessor offices have this kind of information online. It's also readily available through real-estate agents, bankers, lawyers and property appraisers.

Let's say John learns that a four-unit building two blocks away sold two months earlier for $300,000, and another six-unit building around the corner sold for $625,000. Now he knows what ballpark he's playing in. His network will know what rents are in the area, and he can always call landlords and ask what they are charging. They will probably not tell him their expenses, but he can make a reasonable estimate. (Rule of thumb: Operating expenses on larger buildings equal 30 percent to 45 percent of gross rents.)

The apartments in the four-unit building are renting for an average of $700 each, and John figures the owner's expenses are running $1,000 a month. At the six-unit, the rents are $900 with $2,000 in expenses. Cap rates: 7.2 percent at the

MORE NUMBERS

Although the math is different, a cap rate tells a property investor what a price-earnings ratio tells a stock investor. Cap rates and P/Es don't measure the same thing. But they are both widely used benchmarks.

A P/E is the ratio between the price of a stock and the reported per-share earnings of the company. A corporation with a stock price of $40 and earnings per share of $4 and has a P/E ratio of 10/1, or 10. P/Es vary according to how much stock buyers are willing to pay for a claim on future earnings. A high P/E tells you that buyers believe a particular stock can return very high earnings in the future. As I write this, Google's P/E is 92; Citigroup's is 12.

Here are a few other real-estate investors' financial ratios you should familiarize yourself with.

Gross-rent multiplier (GRM). Very important to the seller. You will hear this a lot as sales agents and sellers will cite this figure when showing you properties. "We're asking $400,000. This place generates $38,400 a year income!" It measures the relationship between purchase price and gross income (in this case, GRM = 10.42). That doesn't tell you a lot since it doesn't account for expenses. Still, GRM is a crude rule of thumb that you can learn to use early on in your search. As a buyer, you want a low multiplier; as a seller, you want it higher. The formula: **GRM = price ÷ gross income.**

Debt-service ratio (DSR). Very important to your lender. It's figured by dividing the net operating income by the annual debt payment. The result—which should generally fall in the 1.0 to 1.5 range, depending on the property—is a kind of creditworthiness score that shows whether the building can pay back the loan. A $350,000 building with a net operating income of $38,400 carrying a 30-year $280,000 loan at an interest rate of 6.5 percent will have an annual debt service of $21,120 and a debt-service ratio of 1.8—high, but not unusually so for a smaller property. And high is a good thing, for your lender and for you. All things otherwise being equal, you can count on getting the loan with a higher DSR. The formula: **DSR = net operating income ÷ debt payment.**

Return on investment (ROI). Very important to you. This is your basic scorecard that shows you how your investment is performing. It is different from the cap rate because it includes the interest you pay on your mortgage, which the cap rate does not. If net operating income is $24,000, the mortgage payment is $21,120, and the down payment equals $70,000, the return on investment is 4.1 percent. The formula: **ROI = remaining cash ÷ investment.** A variation, called "total return on investment," can be figured with the total mortgage payment, which includes principal payments: **Total ROI = remaining cash + principal payment ÷ investment;** this becomes more important to you when you sell the building.

❧

four-unit and 6.5 percent at the six-unit. (Note: The smaller building with the lower rents and lower revenue is actually performing better financially than the larger building.)

Now John knows the $400,000 asking price on the four-unit apartment building is too high.

What should he offer? Simple. He wants the best deal he can make, so he divides the net operating income (that's total income minus nonmortgage expenses) by the cap rate he wants. In this case, John would prefer 7.2 percent to 6 percent, right? So he'll lowball a bit, and initially offer $26,000 ÷ .074 = $350,000.

At this point the negotiations become a traditional back-and-forth. The seller counters at $390,000.

"You're killing me," John says.

"You're killing me," the seller replies.

But they strike a deal at $370,000—and a perfectly respectable cap rate in this neighborhood of 7.0 percent.

John agrees to close the deal 60 days after he has concluded his due diligence, including a rigorous inspection of the building and its finances.

GIVE EVERYTHING A HARD LOOK

First thing, John calls his lender, lawyer, accountant and contractor and gets them onboard right away. He'll need their services, and time is essential.

His agreement should include an inspection period (30 days is about right), during which time he should conduct a complete due diligence and thoroughly review the building's finances and its condition.

Few sellers are likely to have their books in the kind of order that you or your accountant would prefer. Like all of us, the seller will have too many receipts just piling up in a shoe box or its equivalent, payments to the local hardware store will have been made with a personal credit card and renters' security deposits will be mingled in the same account as the rent checks. That's not so bad. Accountants see that sort of thing all the time. The important things to look for are that every bit of income, including the tenants' deposits, and every important expense have been or can be documented. And don't fret over the $19 charges at Home Depot; you're looking for the $1,900 in furnace repairs.

You don't want any surprises after you take over the building. If the seller says the air conditioners in apartment 2B were replaced two years ago, trust and verify. Ask to see the receipts.

Have all the paperwork reviewed by your accountant and your lawyer. You pay them to find any problems. You want them to sign off on everything before you take it to your lender as part of your loan application.

Meanwhile, you and the contractor should make arrangements to check out the building itself, including the interior of each apartment. It's the seller's duty to see that the tenants let you in.

At this point, you might also consider writing a short note to each of the tenants introducing yourself, telling them you are considering buying the building, sharing a bit about your plans for it and asking them for any comments or suggestions they may have for the place. (What better sources could you have to learn what's really wrong with the place?)

A new landlord can be scary to tenants, who understandably fear that their rents are likely to be going up and that the way they live is going to be changing. Listen closely to what

INSPECTION CHECKLIST

Here's what you and the contractor should focus on.

- Roof

- Heating and cooling systems

- Plumbing, including leaks beneath the building

- The presence of asbestos, lead paint or other
  hazardous materials

- Electrical systems, including fixtures in the units

- Windows and skylights

- Termites and other infestations

- Floors and carpets

- Laundry room

- Driveways and parking areas

- Landscaping

- Storage areas

- General condition of individual units, including carpets and
  appliances

they tell you, but don't talk about any substantive changes you
are considering. You want to reassure them, not frighten them
further.

The physical inspection is paramount. Wear your rattiest
clothes, and be prepared to walk the roof and crawl around in
the basement beside your contractor. Bring a screwdriver, a
camera, a notebook, a tape measure and maybe some of that

stuff the *CSI* guys spread under their noses before they open the body bags.

You are looking for two things—anything that's wrong with the building now that the seller should fix, and anything that could be a problem after you take over, which you will have to fix. Either way, however, your goal is to see that the seller pays for the major repairs. If it's something he must fix, he'll pay for it out of his pocket. If it's something you will have to fix, you'll try to get the seller to adjust the purchase price to reflect the extra expense.

Again, don't sweat the small stuff. Apartments will always be messier than you would like, hallway lights will be dimmer and something always need painting. You are interested in big-ticket problems that could materially affect your investment.

This will also give you an opportunity to get a handle on your tenants and how they treat their apartments and the building. Recognize the difference between how you live and how they live, and know that tenants have every right to live as they want to in their own homes. It's OK to let the dishes pile up or to leave the bathroom looking like something abandoned by the 101st Airborne. It's not OK to run a meth lab in the kitchen or to warehouse a suspicious cache of flat-screen TVs in the second bedroom.

GET YOUR MONEY

We're keeping things simple here, so we are going to assume that you find no major problems in your inspections of either the finances or the actual building. It is as the seller represented it and as you hoped it would be.

You write up the results of your inspection, including an estimate of whatever repairs your contractor says should be done right away. You include it along with the financial statements in your loan package. Now is the time to formally apply for a loan.

Because you have built a relationship with your lender, you

already know what he is looking for, both in a property and in your application. This, again, will save you considerable time and aggravation during the escrow period. Here are some other documents a lender will want to see from you.

- **Loan application form.** A novice investor, even one buying through a partnership or other corporate structure, will be treated much like a home buyer. Expect to file the usual mountain of intrusive paperwork, including income tax returns, employment verification and personal financial statement.

- **Purchase contract.** This should include all agreements between the buyer and the seller.

- **Financial documents of the building.** This should include the balance and income statements, and the last three years of rent rolls.

- **Leases.** You should expect to show copies of all the tenants' leases.

If you are buying a larger building or are launching a company that will acquire multiple properties, the most important document you will prepare is your business plan.

It's much easier to put together than you probably think. You started writing it in your head the day you first considered real-estate investing. Every step up to now has been a refinement and adjustment to it. Now all you have to do is put it on paper and package it in a professional manner.

You should make your plan in the form of a PowerPoint presentation and put it on a CD as well as your hard drive. Be professional. Print out the PowerPoint pages and include them in a print binder with all supporting material. Make multiple copies of the entire package of material—always keep one for yourself and have at least two that you can leave with every lender you visit.

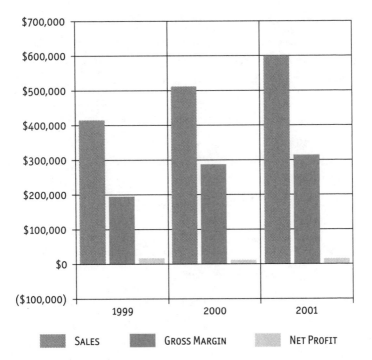

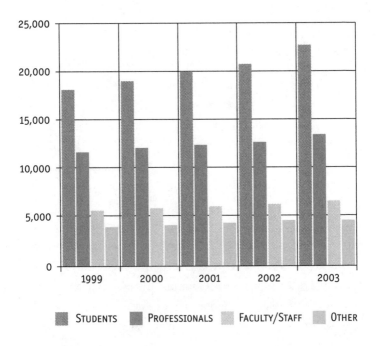

Source: MSN Real Estate, Palo Alto Software, 2006

Business-plan templates are readily available on the Web. One of the most widely used for real-estate investing is called MSN Real Estate by Palo Alto Software. It's a plan for a hypothetical real-estate management and developing firm in Oregon. You follow the template, substituting your own facts and figures for the hypothetical ones.

The program is available at http://www.bplans.com. Here are some sample pages, showing projected income and a market analysis.

Be ready to make a brief oral presentation of the plan, with or without the PowerPoint, if you are asked. Be prepared. Know how to answer any question that might be raised. And always refer the questioner to the appropriate page in the accompanying binder. If you are asked something you don't know the answer to, don't wing it. Say you don't know but will find out and get back to him or her. Be confident. You know you have put together a good deal; now sell it.

We're still assuming that everything has gone smoothly—that you got your loan, you closed the deal and your new tenants love you.

Now it's time for you to meet your new best friend and business partner—the IRS.

CHAPTER 5

WHY THE IRS IS YOUR FRIEND

Government has no other end but the preservation of property.
—JOHN LOCKE

Beginning with a group of landowners writing the Constitution as they eyed a vast, unmapped continent, the government of the United States has long encouraged real-estate investment, speculation and development. Indeed, the only property owners the government ever shafted were the Indians.

That remains as true today as it was 220 years ago. The government may no longer be handing over vast swaths of the West to railroad companies, but it does pick up a substantial portion of the monthly mortgage payments of most homeowners, and it helps landlords trade million-dollar properties, or pass them on to their children, without paying any taxes.

In this chapter, we are going to look at how taxes and government policies encourage real-estate investments and how you, the budding real-estate investor, can take advantage of them. While taxes are a chronic lament of investors everywhere, real-estate investors are among the most blessed when the government comes around for its share of your wealth.

Real-estate loopholes are deeply embedded in the tax laws. It is hard to find a politician who opposes homeowners' mortgage-interest deductions, and a 2005 presidential panel's suggestion to reduce the deduction was as welcome on Capitol Hill as a Gulf Coast hurricane. While it's possible that some day Congress may decide to put some new limits on home-mortgage deductions, even the most radical flat-tax proposals bandied about rarely address fundamental financial concepts such as depreciation or, even more fundamental, the nature of what constitutes business income. All of that is very much to the benefit of landlords and other real-estate investors.

Not that there haven't been rewrites of the laws. Congress changes tax laws all the time, and real estate is frequently affected. In 1997, President Bill Clinton and a heavily Republican Congress gave homeowners one of the greatest tax breaks ever—an exclusion of up to $500,000 of home-sale capital gains (for married couples; $250,000 for singles) that sellers can use every two years when they sell their primary residences.

Twenty years ago, President Ronald Reagan and a largely Democratic Congress closed a number of tax loopholes that had been available to real-estate investors. Prior to that 1986 tax revision, doctors, airline pilots and other high earners flocked to real-estate investments because they could write off all their real-estate losses against regular income. That was the age of the abusive tax shelter, when high earners would "invest" in dubious real-estate ventures simply because they could cut their income taxes.

Back then you had to roll over home-sale proceeds into a new home, but home buying was an even better deal then than it is today because with many two-income families easily reaching into what was then the highest marginal 50 percent tax bracket, the government would pick up half their monthly mortgage-interest payment. There were other tax treats back then, too, like deductions for credit-card interest, and everyone could write off sales taxes. The alternative minimum tax was something only a few very, very rich people had to think about.

No longer. Though still generous, at least by current standards, today's tax breaks and loopholes for real-estate investors are nowhere nearly as advantageous, especially for beginners and relatively small investors. And those doctors and other high earners are pretty much shut out of most typical real-estate tax breaks.

But don't despair. There are still a few goodies for real-estate investors in the tax code. Let's go find some.

INCOME VERSUS EXPENSES

While one of the principal rules of real-estate investing is that no property should ever cost more than it makes, from a tax-paying point of view, that isn't necessarily the case. Tax laws encourage real-estate investors to appear to show losses, even if they are, in fact, making profits.

When it comes to April 15, you want to appear to be just a bit in the red or, at worst, just breaking even. Yes, you want your properties to be paying for themselves, just not by too much. And when it comes to your Form 1040 (Schedule E for landlords), most salaried workers who have real-estate investments on the side likely want to show an actual loss.

Why? Because the government will compensate you for your losses by cutting your taxes.

Congress has granted exceptionally generous tax breaks to real-estate professionals and investors. Real-estate "professionals" can make out like tax bandits, but even part-time investors can enjoy some nice loopholes if they "materially participate" in the managing of their properties. Congress says anyone who makes less than $100,000 a year can deduct as much as $25,000 of "passive activity losses" against regular non-real-estate income.

Let's make this clear: For tax purposes, Congress treats the "earned income" that you receive from your employer as wages or salary differently from the "passive activity income" that you receive from the tenants of your rental properties. Earned income is essentially taxed from the first dollar you make. Yes, there are deductions, but as any employee knows too well, your paycheck arrives with your Social Security, Medicare and income taxes already paid. And once a year, your employer tells the IRS exactly what your before-tax income was, so there will be no misunderstanding and no fudging about how much tax you owe.

But when a tenant hands over a monthly rent check, that's "passive activity income." And there are no deductions ahead of time. And there's no one telling the IRS how much you make. You take all the month's rental money, put it in the bank and then pay your mortgage and monthly bills. Then you set aside some money in your maintenance and contingency fund, pay into your retirement account and pay your health insurance. Only after you have spent all the money on all the things that are arguably related to your rental business ("operating expenses"), do you have any taxable income. And only then must you set aside the money you will need at the end of the quarter for income tax.

Except not really. In addition to all those other deductible expenses, Congress also allows for the phantom "paper" loss of depreciation—a contrived "passive activity loss" that further reduces your taxable income. And if your day job doesn't pay you too much, you can even use the depreciation to cut your income taxes on your regular salary.

For most people, "depreciation" means a loss of value, the decrease over time in the worth of an item such as an automobile, a construction crane or a computer—things that actually get used up or beat up over time, things that are actually worth less after a few years.

But real estate? How does real estate depreciate? It doesn't. Not really.

Even Congress recognizes that land doesn't get used up,

HOW DEPRECIATION WORKS FOR YOU

NONINVESTOR'S INCOME TAX

Gross wages	$80,000
401(k)	($4,800)
Spousal IRA deduction	($2,000)
Adjusted gross income	$73,200
Deductions & exemptions	($15,304)
Exemption deduction	($9,600)
Taxable income	$48,296
Income Tax Due (2005 IRS tax table)	**$6,511**

REAL-ESTATE INVESTOR'S INCOME TAX

Gross wages		$80,000
401(k)		($4,800)
Rental income	$38,400	
Rental expenses (including mortgage interest)	($36,000)	
Depreciation	($9,000)	
Profit/Loss	($6,600)	($6,600)
Spousal IRA deduction		($2,000)
Adjusted gross income		$66,600
Deductions & exemptions		($15,304)
Exemption deduction		($9,600)
Taxable income		$41,696
Income Tax Due (2005 IRS tax table)		**$5,521**

Real-Estate Investor's Tax Savings	**$990**

but it has written the tax laws to allow landlords to depreciate the "improvements" made to the land—buildings, driveways, garages and what goes in or on them.

Of course, foreclosed or other "distressed" properties do lose value in the short term. And certain types of commercial properties might actually decline over long periods of time— think Superfund sites or obsolete factories. But the value of all but the worst properties in the worst neighborhoods rarely goes down over the long term.

Nevertheless, Congress wants to encourage property investment and create housing. So it maintains the fiction of real-estate depreciation as a powerful inducement for individuals

WRITE IT OFF

From a tax-paying point of view, different types of property depreciate over varying lengths of time. There are also different types of depreciation that allow businesses to recover costs at varying time periods.

Under "straight-line" depreciation, the most common form for property investing, owners of residential properties are allowed to write off their buildings over 27.5 years. That is, if a building—just the building, not the land—is worth $275,000, the owner is allowed to depreciate $10,000 a year until the building is totally written off. Commercial property owners must write off over 39 years.

There are separate, faster depreciation schedules for other elements of a rental operation independent of the building itself. So a landlord will have multiple depreciation streams flowing all at once—writing off his building at 27.5 years, appliances and carpets over 5 years and office furniture over 7 years. By the way, if you have any fruit or nut trees on your property, you can write them off over 10 years.

Source: IRS, Instructions for Form 4562

to operate rental properties. It builds in preferences that combined with rental income and actual price appreciation make real estate a far more attractive investment than it might be otherwise. And Congress hasn't stopped there, either. Once delusional, always delusional: Having persuaded themselves that real property depreciates even when they know it doesn't, our elected representatives have devised ways to "recapture" the phantom losses with later taxes. Then, as we will soon see, they manufactured ways to avoid those, too!

So depreciation, simply put, is a valuable subsidy that gives you, the property owner, the right to transfer to other taxpayers a portion of the cost of your investment in a building. You are allowed to use the depreciation write-off to cut your taxable income even if you have actually made money. There are few other investment vehicles so sanctified by the government.

GETTING GOING

Let's see how all this works. We're going to follow one mythical small real-estate investor through a lifetime of investment-property ownership to see how you can use the tax system to your own advantage.

As we follow his progress over a long time, be warned: We are making one very big assumption here—namely, that the tax law stays the same. That's very unlikely, of course, but since we can't guess what Congress will do next, we'll work with the laws we have now.

We're also using round numbers, and keeping the variables to a minimum. In this chapter then, there are no real-estate sales commissions, roofs never need replacing and tenants always pay their rent on time. Income and expenses stay constant.

Nothing's dodgy in this collection of scenarios, by the way. Nothing's going to bring IRS enforcement agents to your home in the middle of the night. Like the saying goes: It's all perfectly legal.

We'll start in 2005. Steve's a 45-year-old married middle manager in New Jersey making a salary of $80,000 a year. He lives with his stay-at-home wife, Iris, and their 5-year-old daughter Maddie in a two-bedroom condo in Hoboken, a charmingly revitalized town just one subway stop across the Hudson River from Manhattan. Steve's a prudent fellow; he bought his condo in 1990 at a small fraction of the cost of similar apartments on the other side of the river. He contributes to his 401(k), Iris has a spousal IRA, and Maddie's college fund is already in five figures.

Steve and Iris also own a nearby four-unit rental building, which Steve bought in 1995 for $350,000, using $70,000 that

INCOME ADJUSTMENTS

If you are a part-time real-estate investor and your "modified adjusted gross income" exceeds $100,000 a year, IRS rules begin phasing out your write-offs of real-estate losses. At $150,000 of income, you lose them completely.

But don't panic. "Adjusted" income is just that. For most salaried people, the adjustments that will make a substantial difference are 401(k) contributions and whatever pretax medical or child-care programs your company may have.

---

his late father left him. Although Steve leaves the stopped toilets and the clogged gutters to a part-time handyman, he drops by two or three days a week to check in on things and spends a few hours each weekend gardening and otherwise puttering around. He personally screens and interviews all potential tenants, and he collects the rents. Iris buys all the supplies, takes charge of apartment decoration, and frequently meets with outside contractors. They split the bookkeeping and other administrative chores.

Between the two of them, they spend 10 hours a week managing the place. So they easily fit into the IRS's definition of "materially participate" in the managing of the building.

The building costs Steve about $36,000 a year to operate, including mortgage payments. Each unit rents for $800 a month, and all the units are rented all year, giving Steve and Iris a gross rental income of $38,400—and a profit of $2,400.

Not good. Because Steve and Iris are such successful and prudent landlords, they could end up paying an additional $360 or more in income taxes.

But the IRS doesn't really want their money. The government would much rather send Steve and Iris a check.

Of the $350,000 Steve paid for the building, the actual structure (excluding the land) was worth $250,000. Steve and

IT'S ALL MATERIAL

For real-estate investors, the key term here is "materially participate." It's the standard by which the IRS determines your tax status and whether you can write off your real-estate losses against other income.

The IRS says (from the instructions of Form 8582cr) that you materially participate if you satisfy one or more of these conditions:

- You worked managing and operating your properties for more than 500 hours in one year.

- The work you did was substantially all of the work that anyone did on your properties.

- You worked for more than 100 hours, and you worked at least as much as anyone else did.

- You have been doing this kind of work for any 5 of the past 10 years.

- Or, based on all the facts and circumstances, you worked on a regular, continuous and substantial basis for at least 100 hours during the year.

Here are a couple of nice kickers: You don't have to do all the work. You and your spouse can combine your participation "even if your spouse did not own an interest in the activity and whether or not you and your spouse file a joint return for the tax year."

And you don't have to maintain especially detailed time records, either. Proof, the IRS says, doesn't require "daily time reports, logs, or similar documents," but can be based on appointment books, calendars or narrative summaries.

IRS bonus: Even less stringent is what the IRS calls "active participation." You still get the $25,000 tax benefit, but the qualifications are less stringent: "You actively participated in a rental real-estate activity if you (and your spouse) owned at least 10% of the rental property and you made management decisions in a significant and *bona fide* sense. Management decisions include approving new tenants, deciding on rental terms, approving expenditures, and similar decisions."

Sources: IRS Publications 527 and 925

Iris can't depreciate the land, but they can depreciate the building itself by any of several formulas, some of which let them "accelerate" the paper losses. We are sticking with straight-line depreciation, according to which they take an annual write-off of about $9,000 ($250,000 ÷ 27.5 years).

Here's why that's a good thing: By including the depreciation paper loss, Steve's $2,400 profit becomes a $6,600 tax loss. He may now deduct that loss from his salaried income, converting what would have been an additional $360 tax bill into a tax refund of about $990.

Let's make this perfectly clear: Steve and Iris make one-third again as much money filing their tax return each year as they do owning and renting their building.

TRADING UP

Believe it or not, the government actually requires real-estate investors to take depreciation. It then requires investors to give one-fourth of the depreciation back in the form of a special 25 percent "recapture" tax when a property is sold. Fortunately for Steve and Iris, the government then bends that rule, too.

Unfortunately, however, Steve and Iris, with just a single small apartment building, are unlikely to accumulate sufficient losses to totally do away with paying anything to the IRS (see "Are You a Professional?" on page 84 to learn how that's done). Still, they can accumulate losses and write them off when they finally sell their building.

But that might not be their best plan. They could instead buy themselves a retirement home and get the government to help them pay for it.

There is another generous loophole Congress and the IRS provide called a "1031 exchange." Simply put, when an investor sells a property, he or she may trade up to a more valuable "like-kind" property without paying taxes on the original sale. There are various complicated hoops the seller must jump through to pull off a 1031 exchange, but it can be very advantageous and financially well worth the procedural hassles.

Here's one way it could play out: Jump ahead 15 years to 2020. Maddie has almost finished college, and Steve, now 60, is planning to retire from his $120,000-a-year human-resources job in five years. Steve and Iris are dreaming of a summer place at their favorite spot on the Jersey Shore. They've even spotted a funky 6,000-square-foot duplex just a block from the boardwalk. The asking price: $600,000. (That breaks down to about $400,000 for the structure, $200,000 for the 50-foot-by-100-foot lot.)

As a part-time landlord, Steve probably hasn't had the good fortune to bank years of phantom losses from his single four-unit rental property. Instead, he and Iris have made good use of their annual paper losses to cut the tax bill on his salary, always keeping it below the $100,000 threshold with 401(k) contributions and other deductions. So Steve expects he'll have to pay taxes when he sells the apartment building for $500,000. He does the math, and figures if he does a traditional sale and then purchase of the new place, he'll pay off what's left of his mortgage loan on the apartment building and end up with about $400,000. But he'll face a tax bill of nearly $80,000—$22,500 on the building's capital gain and another $56,250 on its depreciation recapture.

Wait. Steve can avoid that $80,000 tax bill by structuring a 1031 exchange in which he rolls over the profits of the sale into the new property. That extra money now goes toward the purchase of a new duplex rather than to the government.

Named for its section in the tax code, a 1031 exchange masks a quite simple concept in a mind-numbing array of financial feints and sleights of hand. Arising from the notion that there is no profit to be taxed if an investor sells one investment and then buys another (try that on Wall Street), the 1031 exchange "is the greatest tax shelter left," Doug Stives, a partner at the accounting firm of Curchin & Company in

IT'S A DEAL

In 1031 exchanges, the term "like-kind" is fairly loose. Just about any income or business property will do, even that little place down by the beach, as long as it is "held for productive use in a trade or business or for investment."

That means you can't do a 1031 exchange of your primary home for, say, a retirement condo in Miami Beach—at least not right away—but you can trade your vacant lot in Pasadena for a minimall in Palo Alto.

Here's a quick rundown of possible exchanges, from Asset Preservation, Inc., of Granite Bay, California, a "qualified intermediary" that handles 1031 deals throughout the country.

- Unimproved for improved property

- Commercial building for vacant land

- Duplex for commercial property

- Single-family rental for an apartment

- Industrial property for rental resort property

Red Bank, New Jersey, told my colleague Jonathan Burton of MarketWatch. "The tax law is in your favor because you can sell real estate, roll the gain over into a replacement and never pay tax."

Indeed, a series of properly structured 1031 exchanges could conceivably defer taxes for as long as you live, and then save your heirs taxes, too.

The 1031 transactions are not really exchanges. No one swaps anything. They are, rather, two-step deals in which you sell one property and promptly buy another. The exchange must be executed through a third party—an IRS-approved

TRADING UP WITHOUT PAYING TAXES

ADJUSTED BASIS	Traditional Sale	1031 Exchange
Apartment house purchase (1995)	$350,000	$350,000
Total depreciation taken	($225,000)	($225,000)
Adjusted Basis at Sale	**$125,000**	**$125,000**

GAIN ON SALE		
Sale price	$500,000	$500,000
Adjusted basis at sale	($125,000)	($125,000)
Total gain on sale	$375,000	$375,000
Total depreciation taken	($225,000)	($225,000)
Capital Gain from Appreciation	**$150,000**	**$150,000**

SALE PROCEEDS		
Apartment house sale (2020)	$500,000	$500,000
Mortgage balance	($93,000)	($93,000)
Sale proceeds before tax	$407,000	$407,000
Tax on depreciation recapture (25%)	($56,250)	$0
Capital-gain tax (15%)	($22,500)	$0
Sale Proceeds after Tax	**$328,250**	**$407,000**

1031 Exchange Tax Savings		**$78,750**

"qualified intermediary" (not your attorney or anyone else with whom you have a professional relationship)—who documents the exchange by preparing the necessary paperwork, holds the money and property on your behalf, and structures the sale of the first property and the purchase of the second.

Once the sale closes, you have just 45 days to find a replacement "like-kind" income property of equal or greater value—in the United States only—and six months to close the new deal.

So all Steve needs to do is see that both sides of the beach house are rented out for a while. Two years is probably enough, but since he isn't planning to retire for five years, he may as well keep the place rented as long as he can. Then he and Iris can move in for the summers, keeping their condo in Hoboken and enjoying their own little piece of the shore as well.

Then they can get ready for one final half-million-dollar gift from the government.

CASHING OUT

Steve and Iris chose to keep the whole shore building as a rental until Steve retired in 2025 at age 65. They kept their Hoboken condo but started spending their summers in half of the duplex at the shore.

The monthly nut on the whole place came to just about $2,500 (principal, interest, property taxes and insurance), so they were easily able to cover all their beach-house expenses with seasonal rents on the other half and off-season rents on both units. (They actually made a little profit, but the building's $14,500 a year depreciation took care of that problem.)

When Steve hit age 70, they set on a plan to get rid of the beach house in 10 years. But they knew that if they sold it, they'd face a huge tax bill. So they decided to renovate and expand the place into the sort of house that they had always seen in the fancy shelter magazines—their dream home.

They set out to convert their rental property into their primary residence. They put together a $600,000, two-year budget and hired a hot architect. They spent the two summers of construction in a portion of the house—a 1,000-square-foot, two-bedroom "in-law" unit that they had built as the first phase of the renovation.

They changed their voting registration and got new driver's licenses showing the beach as their primary residence, not the condo in Hoboken. (It's not necessary, but like a real-estate license, just something nice to do if the IRS ever questions you.)

When the house was finished, Steve and Iris moved in. They rented the in-law unit full-time to a local couple for

ARE YOU A PROFESSIONAL?

 The top of the real-estate loophole heap belongs to someone who can call him or herself a real-estate professional. If you meet the IRS requirements, you are not subject to the $150,000 limit on adjusted gross income and are allowed almost unlimited income-tax write-offs from your investment properties.

Let's see how that works. Let's say our real-estate professional has 20 of those four-unit buildings in New Jersey, each with the same numbers as our part-time landlord's one building: $36,000 a year in expenses and $38,400 in rental income. That's an annual profit—income—of $48,000. Not a princely sum, to be sure, but not wildly divergent from the take-home pay (after federal and state taxes, Social Security, Medicare, 401(k) contributions, etc.) of Steve, our part-time landlord, making about $80,000 in salary.

Depreciation on those 20 buildings totals $180,000, totally wiping out the professional's profit (though leaving the $48,000 in his pocket) and carrying over an additional $132,000 in losses to next year and beyond.

Great! Our real-estate professional will probably never pay income taxes again, even when it's time to "recapture" all that depreciation.

Here's what is supposed to happen: Let's say that after 10 years our real-estate professional decides to sell one of his buildings. He has taken $90,000 in depreciation, reducing his "adjusted cost basis" to $260,000. He then sells the building for $500,000, creating a capital gain of $240,000. Of that, the $90,000 of depreciation is "recaptured" at a special 25 percent tax rate ($22,500), while the remaining $150,000 is taxed at 15 percent ($22,500). So our seller owes the IRS $45,000.

But here's what our tax-phobic professional will do in reality. Remember that $132,000 paper loss he has been carrying over and adding to year by year? The IRS allows owners of more than one property to "aggregate" their losses over all their holdings and then carry them for more than a year. So our professional landlord will use $260,000 of his accumulated losses to offset the entire proceeds of the sale.

Our real-estate professional has a very good year. He gets his $48,000 regular income and the entire $240,000, and pays no income tax.

Nice work. And here's how you can get it.

According to the IRS (Publication 925), you qualify as a real-estate professional if more than half of the personal services you performed in all trades or businesses during the tax year were performed in real property trades or businesses in which you materially participated AND you performed more than 750 hours of services during the tax year in real property trades or businesses in which you materially participated.

The term "real property trades or businesses" is quite a catchall, as it encompasses just about anything you could conceivably try doing with a piece of real estate, including, the IRS says, developing or redeveloping it, constructing or reconstructing it, acquiring it, converting it, renting or leasing it, operating or managing it, or brokering it.

One final present: Your spouse can be a real-estate professional while you work another job. The write-offs still work for both of you if you file jointly.

$1,500 a month. They also made arrangements with a local relocation firm to rent out the main portion of the house for $6,000 a month during the September through May off-season whenever a local corporation needed it for use by visitors or transferring executives—on average, about three months a year. During summers, Steve's and Iris's extended family, especially the grandkids, were there all the time.

But too soon, Steve turned 80 in 2040. He and Iris sold the beach house for $1,850,000. More than half—$970,000—was a gain on the sale. But who wants to pay taxes on nearly $1 million?

Fortunately, Steve and Iris didn't have to.

Their wrote off their annual losses and depreciation (remember, the in-law unit that was rented all the time and the main portion of the house was operated as a rental in the off-seasons so Steve and Iris could account for part of the year as if the house was a rental property).

And here's another nice tax break: Like all homeowners,

CASHING OUT ON THE BEACH

ADJUSTED BASIS

Beach house purchase (2020)	$600,000
Beach house renovation (2030)	$600,000
Total depreciation taken	($318,909)
Adjusted Basis at Sale	**$881,091**

GAIN ON SALE

Sale price	$1,850,000
Adjusted basis at sale	($881,091)
Total gain on sale	$968,909
Total suspended losses*	($262,800)
Total depreciation taken	($318,909)
Homeowner's exclusion	($500,000)
Capital Gain from Appreciation	**($112,800)**

SALE PROCEEDS

Beach house sale (2040)	$1,850,000
Mortgage balance	($646,842)
Sale proceeds before tax	$1,203,158
Tax on depreciation recapture (25%)	($79,727)
Capital-gain tax or savings (15%)	$16,920
Sale Proceeds after Tax	**$1,140,351**

*Accumulated "negative" cash flow on rented portions of renovated house, prorated annually

Steve and Iris excluded $500,000 from their gain on the sale because Congress allows all married homeowners filing jointly to take that much out of the sale of a primary residence tax free.

The $500,000 homeowner's exclusion is exceedingly generous and can be used effectively by investors as well as homeowners. You can sell your principal home (not second home) tax free if you have lived in it for two years out of the previous five (or if you are forced to move earlier than two years, you can take a pro rata share, which in most cases is likely to be more than enough to cover your gain). And you need not live in it continuously, either. So provided the shore house was their primary residence, Steve and Iris could spend just five months a year in it every year (5 months × 5 years = 25 months) and still claim it as a primary residence when it came time to sell it.

And homeowners can do it again and again, with every house they live in for at least two years. The tax savings can't be beat. And, as you will see in chapter 6, the homeowner's exclusion can be used quite effectively by investors rehabbing houses—especially the young and hardy ones who are willing to live in a house as they renovate it.

ADDING IT UP

So how did our couple do?

After a 45-year real-estate investing career that began with a $70,000 inheritance in 1995, Steve and Iris ended up with $1,140,000 in their bank account in 2040—a 1,529 percent increase (divided by 45 years, that's a 34 percent average annual return) on their out-of-pocket initial investment of $70,000.

Not bad, but they actually did better. In addition to the increased value of their properties, the couple earned about $380,000 more in rental income than they paid out in mortgage interest and expenses. If you look at Steve and Iris's annual income from the rental properties as comparable to a stock dividend ("yield"), the little four-unit apartment building yielded a steady pretax 3.4 percent each year, a percentage point better than a typical modern stock.

The beach house covered its own costs but never really produced much in the way of annual income. Steve and Iris got a nice second home out of it and a payoff in the end, but little yield since their seasonal rentals covered only the property's expenses and didn't produce any significant profits. (Note: Even Steve and Iris weren't immune to the "a home is not an investment property" rule.) Over the 20 years they owned the beach house, the appreciation came to 2.7 percent a year.

Still Steve and Iris's "total return" (property appreciation plus property income) came to about $1.5 million, a 2,000 percent increase over their $70,000 seed money. Not Microsoft, to be sure, but nothing to sneeze at.

But what about the IRS's contribution? What were all those tax benefits worth to Steve and Iris? From the $1,000 a year that they didn't have to pay because they could write off the apartment-house depreciation against Steve's salary to the 1031 exchange tax deferral to the homeowner's half-million-dollar capital-gain exclusion, tax loopholes pushed their money-in-their-bank-account return up another $183,000. That's money they would have paid in taxes if the government did not favor real-estate investing.

So the bottom line?

Steve and Iris put $1.7 million in their pockets. That's a Warren Buffett–league lifetime total return of 2,330 percent on their $70,000 inheritance.

Uncle Sam, sugar daddy.

LOOSE ENDS

Like the rest of this book, this chapter has been a big-picture account about using the tax laws to your benefit. It should not be taken as the definitive word on the tax advantages of real-estate investments. Nor should you take just my word on how to structure your financial arrangements to take advantage of the tax laws. That's why there are accountants and financial advisers.

Here's a quick rundown of a few other specific tax matters that you may want to consider. Again, remember you should have an accountant for these kinds of things.

Alternative minimum tax (AMT). As more and more middle- and upper-middle-income taxpayers get sucked into this White House–Congress–IRS black hole, real-estate investors can be especially hard-hit as accelerated depreciation and "passive activity losses" are both affected. Even real-estate professionals can be hit.

The first thing you should do about the AMT is write your

senators and representatives and demand they get rid of this thing. And if they don't do anything about it, fire them and find someone who will.

In the meantime, stick to straight-line depreciation. And you may want to consider setting up a corporate entity (such as an S or C corporation) to hold and manage your properties. That can raise another set of issues and corporate taxes can be high indeed, but at least the AMT-denied passive losses can be characterized as business losses, which are allowed.

Dealer or developer? Know what business you are in. The IRS labels real-estate investors. As you know, the label "professional" is good; "dealer" and "developer" are less good. A professional is someone whose principal business is real estate, and he or she has virtually unlimited write-offs against outside income. But if you do a lot of buying and selling of properties in a given year (think of a shopkeeper and his buying and selling of his inventory), the IRS will consider you a dealer engaged in the "trade or business" of real estate and subject to self-employment taxes. That's 15 percent off the top, just like a wage earner.

Developers, including people who regularly rehab properties, have their own tax issues. Depreciation is restricted until a property is "put in service," which means no write-offs during construction. And since the properties are made to be sold right away, there are no opportunities for depreciation after construction, either. Also, if you buy, rehab and sell a property in less than a year, you will pay regular income tax on the proceeds of the sale rather than the lower capital-gains taxes. There are also rules that require developers to capitalize many day-to-day costs of doing business. That, too, will greatly limit write-offs.

Death. Federal estate taxes currently are being phased out (though they are scheduled to return in 2010). It is likely Congress will fashion some kind of estate tax if it ever again seriously tries to balance the government's books. (Dead people don't vote.) And states are still likely to maintain estate taxes even if the federal government doesn't. As you should with all investments, structure your real-estate holdings in order to minimize estate taxes.

Facing a loss on your primary residence? This can be the sad result of buying a new home amid a rapid run-up of prices and then selling it in a downturn. You may not be able to get all your money out. You are not allowed to take a tax loss on your residence.

So rent it out. Unless you absolutely, positively cannot afford to move without selling, you should rent your home for at least two years after you move out. Then sell it. Congress's heart may turn to stone when it comes to desperate home-owners in the aftermath of a housing bubble, but real-estate investors are another matter. After you have had the home in rental service for a couple of years, Congress will allow you to deduct capital losses and "suspended losses" at the time you sell it (the decline in value and any negative cash flows). You can then take the loss on your home converted to a rental property against your ordinary income.

Home-office deduction. Don't bother. More than 1.5 million people do take a home-office deduction. But unless your office is a big part of your house, it's not worth it, and it's not worth putting a neon sign on your tax return that says, "Hey, IRS, look here!" Here are the quick numbers: You are already deducting your mortgage interest, so if you have a 4,000-square-foot house with a 200-square-foot office, you can deduct just 5 percent of the monthly principal. That's probably no more than about $20 on a $300,000 note. Maybe you get another $20 on utilities.

Better plan: If you have to have a place to work, go rent yourself an office. It will give you someplace to go as well as a cleaner tax return, and you can use the home-office space for your model-train layout.

Method of holding. You want to own your properties so you can minimize any potential tax issues. There is good reason to have a separate entity own each of your properties: You minimize your liability in lawsuits that way. But that won't necessarily reduce your income or estate taxes.

If it's you and your wife or other family member who own the property, you want to own it as a "joint tenancy," which gives the surviving partner full ownership upon the death of the other partner. (If your state permits it, you and your wife may want to hold the title as "community property.") If you and an unrelated partner (or someone you don't want to pass it on to) own a property together, you want to hold it as "tenants in common." That means your half belongs to you and is part of your estate; your partner's half belongs to him and his estate. If you form a company to hold your properties, you want similar ownership arrangements for the corporate entity.

Retirement-fund investing. This became attractive during the real-estate bubble. If you want a real-estate component in your traditional IRA, stick to real-estate investment trusts and other publicly traded real-estate investments—real-estate developing and operating companies that, you guessed it, enjoy a special tax status. There's no tax advantage to placing properties in a traditional individual retirement account, as you lose even the capital-gains preference and pay the full-rate income tax when you sell and later take an IRA distribution.

Sophisticated investors might be able to make use of a tax-free Roth IRA, however. Owners of a Roth IRA put in after-tax money, which then grows tax free, and you never have to pay income tax when you take money out. Properly structured, then, real estate held in a Roth could end up generating no tax liabilities at all.

Social Security and Medicare. Here's another big gift from the government. Landlords are exempt from Social Security and Medicare taxes. Rental income isn't considered "earned income," so there are no payroll or self-employment taxes on the owner's income. Of course, that means you won't qualify for Social Security or Medicare benefits if you are a full-time landlord your entire working life. But if your rental operation supplements your salaried income, you could retire with the best of both worlds—government retirement benefits and sizable savings.

"What if I'm audited?" There's nothing in this book that's illegal or that will bring the IRS hammer down on you. And you shouldn't do anything unless you have run it past your accountant. Those caveats aside, don't sweat your taxes because (1) you're an honest person, (2) you keep good records and (3) the IRS's bark is far worse than its bite.

Your chances of being audited in the first place are minuscule—less than 1 percent of all returns are pored over. And audits come in all sorts of shapes and sizes, most of which involve merely the questioning of one particular item on your return. And a dreaded full audit is so rare that you'd profit far more worrying about global warming.

Let's get real. The tax-bemoaning rhetoric so often heard from real-estate investors is way overwrought. Like all businesspeople, they are on far stronger footing with the IRS than any salaried man or woman whose annual earnings are reported to the IRS on a W-2 form. It's you, the landlord, not an employer, who tells the IRS what you received in rent, what expenses you paid, what you actually made and what taxes you owe.

Honesty goes a long way. Report all your income; report your expenses. As long as you don't grossly understate your income or grossly overstate your expenses—that is, as long as you stay within the bounds of believability and reason—the IRS is pretty much going to take your word for it.

CHAPTER 6

There's No Place Like a Home

Smaller Residential Investment Properties

In no other country in the world is the love of property keener or more alert than in the United States.

—Alexis de Tocqueville

The odds are that your first investment property will be a house or a small apartment building. They are cheaper for one thing, and easier to manage. They are where you can learn the basics of property investing without getting in over your head. And they are the basis for any well-rounded investment property portfolio.

In this chapter, we are going to look at different types of smaller residential investment properties, weighing the pros and cons of each. We've grouped these because they all offer the possibility for owner financing, just like a single-family home. We will look at larger residential and commercial properties in the next chapter.

As we noted in chapter 4, you do want the best building you can find in the best neighborhood. But even that is subject to more interpretation than you may think. What's a good neighborhood for one tenant may be totally uninteresting to another. So a good neighborhood depends on who you expect to be renting your building.

A trendy in-town neighborhood with a Starbucks or two and lots of rehabbed Victorian town houses may be very attractive to young singles (and, increasingly, older empty nesters), but young families are much more likely to be interested in traditional Ozzie-and-Harriet suburban-style neighborhoods with lots of single-family homes and good schools. The young singles will probably pay a higher percentage of their incomes for fashionable addresses, but they may be prone to move more often than families. The families are apt to be a bit more cost conscious as they pay rent and struggle to save for buying their own homes.

Once again, you should try to focus your efforts, asking yourself these questions: What kind of business do I want to be in? What kinds of properties do I want to own?

Let's explore some options.

IN-LAW UNITS

The most basic form of property investment is a so-called in-law unit or guesthouse that sits on the site of your home itself, sometimes as a separate building, sometimes attached to the main house. No one has ever gotten rich renting out such properties, but they can significantly reduce the cost of homeownership.

Between World War II and the 1980s, there were relatively few homes built with such units. The postwar suburban ideal of the nuclear family living in a single-family home sitting on its own lot surrounded by hundreds of other single-family homes on their own lots simply didn't allow for such arrangements. Quite common before the postwar housing boom—when they were often called "servants' quarters"—small extra

SMALLER RESIDENTIAL PROPERTIES

All of the properties discussed in this chapter are appropriate for novice investors.

Property Type	Pros	Cons
In-law units	Easy to operate and manage; good for personal cash flow; compelling financial benefits	Living in close quarters with your renter; possible zoning problems
Weekend or vacation homes	Significantly cuts second-home costs; two weeks of tax-free income	Sharing your living space with renters; losing some prime-time vacation time; tax issues
Single-family homes	Single-family homes are always in demand; relatively easy to maintain; easy to finance; good supply of properties	Extreme price increases in some areas recently; pool of renters diminished as many renters became first-time homeowners; cash flow dependent on single property; risky to flip in the current environment
Duplexes and small apartment homes	Extremely attractive pricing; neighbors pay for your home; virtually all expenses can be written off; "smoother" cash flow with more than one rental unit; easy financing	Sharing your private space with tenants; on-site landlord

living spaces became fashionable again with the rise of the New Urbanism movement that has tried to re-create the look and cultural texture of prewar America. Today, some otherwise very traditional postwar-style suburban developments are featuring the additional units, which are often pitched by developers as housing for aging parents or 20-something children returning to the nest. Whatever the stated purpose of the extra units, homeowners have long netted themselves extra income by renting them out.

Of course, local laws dictate what homeowners can do with these properties, and in towns with strict land-use policies you may be legally barred from renting out the in-law unit. The good news is that many towns and cities are far more agreeable to such arrangements today than they were 10 or 15 years ago and will issue the necessary "certificate of occupancy" to legalize the arrangement.

That said, however, it's hardly unknown for people to ignore the spirit of regulation by adhering strictly to the law that allows "nephews" or "nieces" or "cousins" to live in the extra apartments. ·

Warning: Even if you are renting your unit on the sly, be sure to adhere to state and federal tax laws. Some states, for instance, require the sales taxes be paid on rental units. The worst tax mistake anyone can make is to have undeclared income. On the income front, honesty always pays.

That caveat aside, the numbers behind an in-law unit can be compelling. Anything you can do to reduce your own monthly housing nut is, quite literally, money in your pocket. At current interest rates, the monthly payment on a $350,000 30-year mortgage is $2,200 a month; taxes, insurance and maintenance can easily push that up another $500 or much more, depending on your location. Do the math: Over the course of that 30-year mortgage, the homeowner will pay $796,000 in principal and interest alone. Renting out an in-law unit for just $400 a month and using that money every month to pay down principal will shave 10 years from the mortgage term and reduce total payments by more than $165,000.

And, as we saw in chapter 5, the savings don't have to stop there. With just one in-law unit, you will probably not qualify under the IRS's material-participation rules. But you will be able to write off all your costs—including depreciation on the unit itself along with appliances and other furnishings—up to your actual rental income. So you probably won't end up paying any income tax on your bonus income, and you will end up paying a big piece of your mortgage principal with untaxed money. And a legal unit should boost the resale value of a house to reflect the income the unit produces.

WEEKEND OR VACATION HOMES

For many second-home owners, a weekend house is an indulgence, something that's nice to have and provides a great deal of psychic pleasure. There are few moments more sublime than sitting on your own porch overlooking the lake or the ocean with all the hassles and woes of your workaday world shunted far back in your consciousness.

And there are few moments more depressing than when, at the end of the month, as you pay the school tuition, the car note, the day-care center and all the other bills, you have to pay the vacation-house mortgage, the utilities, the caretaker and the complete set of other bills that come from operating a second household. Yes, you could probably check into the Ritz-Carlton every weekend for what that damn place is costing you.

That's when second-home owners invariably decide they really should rent the place out. And for many people, their first foray into property investing and management will come when they rent out the weekend place.

Just as with an in-law unit, renting out your weekend house is not a way to get rich. At best, it's another way to manage your personal cash flow and to reduce your monthly nut. Many of the same numbers that applied in our discussion of in-law units can be applied to your weekend home, although the tax situation is decidedly different. Yes, you could probably rent it out full-time and make a real profit, but that would defeat the purpose, would it not? If you don't have use of your second home, why have one at all?

The negatives of renting your vacation home invariably fall on those psychic issues as much as the financial ones. After all, it's one thing to rent out a separate residence that happens to be attached to your private home and another matter altogether to rent out your home itself on a weekend basis. If you

SUN BURNED

Until the most recent price run-ups, the rule of thumb for a week's rental of a vacation home in a popular seasonal tourist area was one week equals one month of expenses. As the prices for places in popular resorts skyrocketed, that rule went the way of affordable oceanfront condos—a sure sign in itself of the mania that overtook many real-estate markets in the last few years.

As of this writing, the asking price for a peak-season rental of a $700,000 Gulf-front, three-bedroom Panama City, Florida, condo is now as much as $4,200 a week. That's a lot of money, but once you figure in the cost of vacant weeks, an 80 percent jumbo mortgage, monthly association fees, property taxes, rental agent's commission and other associated expenses, the condo owner is probably not breaking even.

Furthermore, vacation condos rarely qualify for rental-tax preferences. The material-participation bar is too high for an absentee owner who needs on-site maintenance and management services.

can't comfortably share your actual living space—your weekend renters will eat off your plates, sleep in your beds, sit on your porch and, from time to time, break your things—you are not psychologically cut out to operate your weekend house as a rental.

If, however, you can take those kinds of things in stride, then you can make a nice dent in your second-home expenses just by renting it a few weeks or weekends a year. If your weekend home is in an area with a strong seasonal attraction, such as Cape Cod or the skiing towns of Colorado, you will probably have to give up some prime time in order to maximize your rental income. An area with year-round appeal, of course, offers rental opportunities in times of the year when you won't want to be there yourself. Some second-home owners do manage to make a nice business renting in off-seasons. If your lake house happens to be in or near a college town, for example, you can rent the house during the school year at a very reasonable monthly rent to teachers or students (though be careful with the latter).

Perhaps the most daunting aspect of renting your weekend home is the income-tax issue. First, the IRS gives second-home landlords a very nice little present in that it allows two weeks of tax-free rental income a year. You can make a small dent in your expenses just doing that. For many second-home owners, that's enough right there.

Beyond that, however, the accounting can be irksome. The IRS doesn't want people buying second homes and disguising them as rental properties. It has two criteria to determine whether the property is a second home (bad) or a rental (good). It's a second home if you don't rent it out at all or if you personally use it at least two weeks a year or 10 percent of the number of days the place is available for rental, whichever is longer.

All this means, of course, is that you are not likely to get the full real-estate tax benefits of the second home. You can still rent it out, however, and, like an in-law unit, write off the income against expenses.

SINGLE-FAMILY HOMES

Throughout much of the country, the market for single-family homes is seriously out of whack. The real-estate bubble sent prices so high that they outstripped the ability of single-family properties to generate rental income sufficient for landlords to cover their mortgage and operating costs. Indeed, in many of the largest metropolitan areas it is far better for your personal monthly cash flow to be a tenant and rent a house than to be an owner and buy one.

Not that anyone seems to be noticing. The recent increases in homeownership rates and prices have been stunning. In 2005, 69 percent of households owned their homes, up from

64 percent a decade ago. That's roughly half a million new homeowners every year. Likewise, the median price for a single-family home hit $219,000 in 2005, according to the National Association of Realtors. That was up from just $107,000 in 1995.

In short, this is not a great time for bargain shoppers, and buying bargain properties is the best way to make money in this real-estate niche. You can do it in one of two ways: Renting or "flipping." Renting is a classic "buy-and-hold" strategy, while flipping calls for quick turnarounds of fixer-upper properties that can be spruced up and sold quickly. Either can be appropriate for novice investors, but both require acquiring properties at significantly reduced prices.

Michael Bremser, a high-tech engineer and real-estate investor in Southern California, has been taking his money off the table lately. He is significantly reducing his exposure to local real estate because prices have just reached too high.

"Single-family homes have worked pretty well for me," he says, "but we're moving away from them because prices have gone up so much that you can't even find places that are cashflow positive."

So it would be tempting here to say hoard your cash and hang on. Avoid this segment of the market unless you have a chance to buy a property at a 30 percent or 40 percent discount from its previous price.

Don't think this is out of the question. In the late 1980s and early 1990s, when the government set up the Resolution Trust Corporation to liquidate the real-estate loan portfolios of bankrupt savings-and-loan institutions, speculators picked up properties for just dimes on the dollar. The air is escaping the bubble, interest rates are on the rise, and with the next economic downturn there is likely to be an abundance of foreclosed single-family properties available at prices attractive to property investors.

RENTING

Renting houses is the simplest and, long term, the more prudent of the two strategies. It's basic stuff, but it can be very difficult, if not impossible, to make a house pay for itself at current inflated prices and at typical loan-to-value ratios. That's because if your house carries an 80 percent or 90 percent loan, the renter will have to pay more per month to rent the house than he would to buy it. That may work for dumb rich people taking a beach house in the Hamptons or a Manhattan penthouse, but it's not going to fly for long with any tenant who can add and actually works for a living.

Look at it this way: There's a handsome three-bedroom, two-bath house in the 33635 zip code of Tampa, Florida, for sale at an asking price of $199,900. If you bought it with 10 percent down and a 90 percent loan at 6 percent, your monthly payment will be just about $1,550 (that's PITI—principal, interest, taxes and insurance). As a landlord, at a bare minimum, you'll want to budget at least $200 a month in additional expenses, including lawn upkeep, water, repairs and cash reserves.

That puts your break-even point at almost $1,800 a month. That's far more than you can reasonably expect to earn where comparable properties in the same neighborhood can be rented for less than $1,300. You'd face a negative cash flow of $6,000 a year! And forget about the depreciation. Just to break even, you'd have to put down about $80,000 (40 percent) on this property. That will buy you no income and, assuming modest 3 percent annual appreciation, a lackluster long-term return.

You should probably pass on this real-estate opportunity . . . unless you can get it for a lot less money. And the best way to do that is buying foreclosure houses or houses that have gone through some type of government seizure.

There are plenty of books and articles about buying foreclosures and other distressed properties so we'll keep it broad here. You can make some nice money picking up single-family homes for just a fraction of their previous values. You must be smart and quick, however. This is not an area that is easily gotten into, as novice investors are usually many steps behind more sophisticated players.

People such as Ron and Cathy Tucker. They are attracted to properties in the worst shape—even condemned houses— that they can buy for less than $50,000, spend that much to fix and then rent or sell. Generally, they borrow money on their other income properties in order to finance their rehabbing. They concentrate their efforts in older, close-in Tampa neighborhoods of smaller houses built in the 1920s and 1930s.

Lately, they've been eyeing a place that few novices would think has any potential at all—a burned-out shell of a wood-frame house. (Look up and you can see the sky, look down and you can see the dirt.) But what looks like a daunting prospect to a novice is a big opportunity to Cathy. She and Ron have built new houses in the past, so she knows what to expect, and that, in part, is why the virtual teardown was so attractive. In a word: permits.

"This place already has a sewer connection. It already has electricity," explains Ms. Tucker, as she ticks off the months and layers of local property bureaucracy that most builders have to go through to build a new house. But buying this shell will bypass all that, saving time and money on the project. So when she finishes the building project, her costs will be lower, which means she will be able to rent or sell the virtually all-new house at a bigger profit.

Without a track record in acquiring distressed properties, you are not likely to pull off something like the Tuckers' plan. But you can find deals and make some money.

Let's stay in the Tampa area, but go back to that three-bedroom, two-bath house we saw earlier. Remember, it was priced too high to justify buying it as income property. You're not likely to get the seller to come down enough to make it profitable. But it turns out that there's a very similar house available less than a mile away. This other house is roughly the same size with the same three bedrooms and two baths. The difference is this one's being taken over by its lender.

Tampa's Hillsborough County is digitally up to date; it has all kinds of public records online that anyone, anywhere, can visit for free. And there's the house right there on the clerk's *lis pendens* list, which is just Latin for "litigation pending." It's where the first official document in an impending foreclosure shows up. (Go to the county court clerk at http://www.hillsclerk.com and click on "online records search." For tax liens, by the way, visit http://www.hillstax.org.)

This particular house has a mortgage loan of $110,000. Knowing only that, the numbers all of a sudden look much different and much more favorable to a future landlord. Sophisticated buyers of foreclosed properties know that they, not the homeowner who is facing financial ruin nor the lender about to take over the property, are usually in the driver's seat on such potential acquisitions. A buyer with cash who is ready to make a deal can drive a hard bargain and make out very well. And the worse the market, the better for the buyer.

That's because by this point both the delinquent homeowner and the mortgage holder are over barrels. The homeowner is three months behind on his mortgage payments and could well be out of work and behind on lots of other bills as well. The house is getting shabbier daily as the owner saves money by not fixing things and not maintaining the lawn. He has probably been trying to sell the house and get his remaining equity out but can't find a buyer. (Even in a booming market, buyers can be hard to find for properties that are falling into disrepair. In down markets, there are no buyers at all—except investors.) He is growing more desperate daily.

Meanwhile, the lender has already lost at least three months of payments on this loan and now must wait out the homeowner for an additional three to six months before it will be allowed to take over the property, after a public auction at which it will bid the value of the mortgage note. At that point, the lender will take over the house, evict the former owner, pay for a quick fix-up, hire a real-estate broker and put it on the market—where, as you already know, the lender can ask no more than $200,000.

In other words, this lender is facing a year or more of lost income (at least $6,000), taxes and insurance (about $3,000), rehab costs ($15,000), broker's fees ($12,000) and ongoing taxes, utility charges and maintenance expenses (at least $400 a month). And unlike a homeowner or a landlord, the lender-owner facing losses can neither live in the house nor rent it out. This lender—$36,000 in the hole and preparing to write off the loss—wants out.

That gives you, the potential buyer, considerable clout with both the delinquent homeowner and the lender. But at this stage, you'll want to approach the homeowner. It will take some schmoozing, but your goal is to persuade the owner to sell you the property for as little as possible.

The best deal you can expect with the homeowner is to acquire the building for the cost of making the owner whole with the lender and any others with liens against the property— mainly the accumulated missed payments, just a couple of thousand dollars at this point. This is called a "subject-to" purchase, and it must be approved by the principal lender. (Although most mortgage contracts include "due-on-sale" clauses that require full repayment of the loan upon transfer to a new owner, many lenders will work with buyers who step in at this stage.)

If others are competing to acquire the property, which they usually are, you might find yourself in a bidding situation. If you are determined to acquire the property, you will need to sweeten the offer and pay some money above the missed payments. Be careful. Don't get carried away. Your goal is to acquire the property at a price that will make it pay for itself.

If you simply make the owner whole and take over an existing 90 percent or 95 percent note, you won't make any money. Let the place go into foreclosure. The lender will most

FINDING FORECLOSURES

Freddie Mac (Federal Home Loan Mortgage Corporation) and Fannie Mae (Federal National Mortgage Association) both maintain extensive "REO" (real-estate owned) property lists, as does the Department of Housing and Urban Development (HUD). Other federal agencies, including the Treasury Department and Department of Agriculture, also maintain lists of properties for sale or auction.

In addition, just about every large mortgage lender maintains REO lists that can be accessed through their Web sites. You'll have to root around, but the lists are there. Here are some examples.

- http://bankofamerica.reo.com/search/

- http://www.bankone.com/answers/BolReoSearch.aspx

- http://www.citimortgage.com/RetailTools/oreo/SearchListing.do

- http://www.countrywide.com/purchase/f_reo.asp

- http://www.homesteps.com/hm01_1featuresearch.htm

- http://www.hud.gov/homes/index.cfm

- http://www.mortgagecontent.net/reoSearchApplication/fanniemae/

- http://www.treas.gov/auctions/customs/realprop.html

likely take over the property at a foreclosure auction since no one is likely to bid more than the mortgage value. Then low-ball the lender.

Recognize that a foreclosed property is a lender's failure, and the managers want to get rid of it. Once the lender has taken over the property and evicted the former owner, it will place the property with the "REO" (real-estate owned) department for disposal. It will be listed with a local broker and put up for sale, usually at a price that will recoup the bank's losses but is still attractively lower than comparable nearby properties. Typically, the bank will offer the property "as is," which usually means it will not fix anything wrong. That is negotiable, however, especially if problems involve environmental hazards such as asbestos or lead paint.

In a falling or stagnant real-estate market, you should be able to get it for even less. A bank will entertain any reasonable offer and, depending on the property, perhaps even some unreasonable offers. Remember, your goal is to get the house at a fire-sale price—30 percent to 40 percent below value, or better.

FLIPPING, REHABBING AND RENOVATING

If you are determined to flip your way through whatever may be left of the boom, the best way is finding derelict, abandoned or otherwise undesirable properties in the very best neighborhoods or in up-and-coming parts of town, rehabbing them and then selling them. You may not make a great deal of money doing this, but it will let you play what's left of the boom. Speed is essential. You don't want to be left holding a property that you can't sell.

That's what happened to Lisa Clark, who took a stab at rehabbing "in one of the most expensive zip codes in America"—Rancho Santa Fe, California, a seven-square-mile enclave of multimillion-dollar homes in San Diego County. Ms. Clark ended up holding on to one of those million-dollar properties far longer than she had hoped or planned.

Early in 2005, Ms. Clark bought the "last, best dump" in town, a 1,460-square-foot $700,000 two-bedroom, two-bath condo and then rejected her real-estate agent's advice to "repaper it and flip it." Ms. Clark: "I took a look and said, 'This has to be made into a residence that's appropriate for the caliber of lifestyle people here are used to.'"

Ms. Clark fashioned a library/media room out of a dining alcove, built a formal dining room where the kitchen had been

MANAGING THE RISK

Clearly, the biggest drawback to single-family home flip deals in this housing climate is the risk involved—especially in a market that is topping out. You simply don't know what the market will look like a year or two out. All you know about interest rates is they are likely to rise. And you don't know what kind of shape the economy will be in or what the local employment picture will be like. You need to minimize your risk as much as possible. Here are a couple of ideas.

Get a partner. Under the 50 percent of something beats 100 percent of nothing rule, consider sharing the wealth. Or more precisely, get someone else to share their wealth with you.

Presell. Have proper architectural drawings made showing what the finished house will look like and then try selling the place during construction. Professional developers do this all the time. Remember, buyers get caught up in manias, too, so they could see a bargain in an "under-construction" price.

Plan B. Like Colin Powell, always have an exit strategy. Keep your expenses in check so that you can afford to rent the place—or live in it yourself—if you have to. Be prepared to renegotiate your loans if you are going to have trouble making payments. If the overall economy has gone bad, then lenders will be more helpful. If your mortgage and construction loans are with the same lender, the bank's exposure will be so great that it will be eager to work with you to keep the property out of foreclosure. Worst case: Study the new federal bankruptcy law.

and put in a new kitchen in place of an old family room. She filled the new kitchen with top-of-the-line appliances and put in some fancy, if not overly expensive, furniture.

In September 2005—after she learned that her first contractor had been running up bills at Home Depot for unrelated products and a second one lost interest in the project before it was finished and she had hired a third to wrap things up—Ms. Clark was finally able to put the place up for sale. Asking price: $1.5 million. "The real-estate market in California just stopped," she laments. She gave up her own rental apartment and moved into the new place with her daughter. In January, she lowered her asking price to $1.375 million. Still no takers.

"I would not recommend that for someone getting started flipping homes," Ms. Clark says. "Guys who do this put in $20,000 or $30,000, stick to fixing things people look for, and keep their carrying time to 45 to 60 days.

"I've put in $225,000. I'm about as stretched as you can be and have taken about as large a risk as you could."

Such experiences should not deter you, but they should give you pause. This is risky business in an unpredictable market. Still, let's look at how it can be done by taking a hypothetical stab at flipping a place in one of the most overheated markets in the country—San Francisco.

Decide where you want to buy and for how much. In the current climate, it is going to be very difficult to find a house, in any condition, that is for sale at the kind of discount you want—at least 20 percent below comparable renovated properties, or better, 30 percent or 40 percent below. One thing to keep in mind: You often hear about the "median" house price in a given area. Well, remember the median is where half the properties sell above that mark and, more important, half sell below. So even in infamously expensive San Francisco, there are going to be properties available for well under the local $650,000 median. Those are properties that have the potential at least of making you some money.

A simple search on Realtor.com found 113 underpriced San Francisco houses in the summer of 2005. Prices started at $399,000 for an 800-square-foot, one-bedroom, one-bath house—the cheapest listed house in the city. The owners of two-bedroom houses (1,000 to 1,300 square feet) in the same general neighborhood were asking in the mid-to-high $700,000s.

So your question as a potential renovator and property

flipper is, can I afford the house at this price and then renovate it and enhance the value enough to justify a much higher
sales price?

For the kind of job this place will take, you should be looking about two years out, determining the value of the place
then, not just now. Prices in the first half of the decade rose 15
percent a year in San Francisco, so you would estimate a 30
percent price increase between mid-2005 and mid-2007. That
would put the value of today's $750,000, 1,300-square-foot, two
bedroom, two-bath houses at about $925,000 in 2007. Be con-
servative in your planning: In this climate, figure your expenses as if the price rise will be just 15 percent, or to about
$860,000. To be really conservative and prudent, run your
numbers at a $750,000 price and again at 10 percent below
that, or $680,000. If you do better and sell for a higher price,
hooray for you.

At the $860,000 sales price, you can still project a healthy
return on investment of 54 percent—that's your profit divided
by all expenses. You are going to want to raise the overall
square footage of the house and the number of bedrooms and
baths. Your architect, contractor and you plan a gut renovation
of the existing house, a major upgrade of the kitchen, and a
500-square-foot addition. You estimate it will take 18 months
and cost about $175 a square foot to do what you want to do—
about $225,000. You will need a 90 percent loan-to-value loan
to buy the place and another loan to handle the construction.

Banks do make those kinds of loans today. It's quite risky,
of course, as your payoff won't come for another year and a
half or two years. Your total costs will be high, and you are hoping for continued rapid and substantial price increases. And
as you can see from the spreadsheet on page 110, your margin
for error is narrow. You can expect to make a profit only if
prices continue to rise as they have in the past.

Still, it can be done.

Obviously, your profit picture will improve for every dollar that you can increase the sale price or reduce the costs. The

FLIPPING A SAN FRANCISCO HOUSE 1

Estimated Sale Price	**$925,000**	**$860,000**	**$750,000**	**$680,000**
Real-estate commission	($55,500)	($51,600)	($45,000)	($40,800)
Incidental sales costs	($10,000)	($10,000)	($10,000)	($10,000)
Mortgage loan payoff	($359,000)	($359,000)	($359,000)	($359,000)
Construction loan payoff	($225,000)	($225,000)	($225,000)	($225,000)
Gross Profit	**$275,500**	**$214,400**	**$111,000**	**$45,200**
Down payment	($40,000)	($40,000)	($40,000)	($40,000)
Incidental acquisition costs	($5,000)	($5,000)	($5,000)	($5,000)
Two-year property taxes	($10,000)	($10,000)	($10,000)	($10,000)
Insurance and other ownership costs	($12,000)	($12,000)	($12,000)	($12,000)
Interest payments on mortgage:	($48,000)	($48,000)	($48,000)	($48,000)
Interest payments on construction loan:	($24,000)	($24,000)	($24,000)	($24,000)
Total expenses	($139,000)	($139,000)	($139,000)	($139,000)
Net Pretax Profit (loss)	**$136,500**	**$75,400**	**($28,000)**	**($93,800)**
Return on Investment (net profit ÷ expenses)	**98%**	**54%**	**−20%**	**−67%**

basic business plan included the opportunity for a substantially higher sale price, but where can you cut your expenses?

If you have a real-estate license, you can expect to cut the sales commission by as much as half. You could conceivably save all the commission by handling the sale entirely yourself, but you can't count on that. You don't want to shut out other agents who might have a buyer ready to deal. Another area where you might be able to shave some costs is the purchase price—probably not a lot in this market, but some (say, $10,000).

You can also shave a lot of the construction costs by doing work yourself. First, if you are drawn to this sort of investment in the first place, you probably have better-than-average fix-it skills to begin with. Then there are plenty of jobs around any construction site that just about anyone can do, from cutting and stapling insulation battens to hanging drywall to tiling and painting. Save the expensive stuff for the pros, but you should be able to trim at least 10 percent of the construction costs by doing work yourself and cutting back on some amenities.

Just these very minor adjustments make a substantial difference to the bottom line of the project. The projected return on investment is now 98 percent—doubling your money in just two years. And you can see why serious property flippers are always on the lookout for properties way below prevalent market prices. A more experienced flipper might even make a substantial profit on this building if prices stagnate or even fall.

Finally, a very big potential savings can come in how you own the place. If you buy the house as your principal residence, not only will you get a slightly better mortgage interest

FLIPPING A SAN FRANCISCO HOUSE 2

Estimated Sale Price	**$925,000**	**$860,000**	**$750,000**	**$680,000**
Real-estate commission	($26,000)	($26,000)	($26,000)	($26,000)
Incidental sales costs	($10,000)	($10,000)	($10,000)	($10,000)
Mortgage loan payoff	($349,000)	($349,000)	($349,000)	($349,000)
Construction loan payoff	($200,000)	($200,000)	($200,000)	($200,000)
Gross Profit	**$340,000**	**$275,000**	**$165,000**	**$95,000**
Down payment	($40,000)	($40,000)	($40,000)	($40,000)
Incidental acquisition costs	($5,000)	($5,000)	($5,000)	($5,000)
Two-year property taxes	($10,000)	($10,000)	($10,000)	($10,000)
Insurance and other ownership costs	($12,000)	($12,000)	($12,000)	($12,000)
Interest payments on mortgage:	($48,000)	($48,000)	($48,000)	($48,000)
Interest payments on construction loan:	($24,000)	($24,000)	($24,000)	($24,000)
Total expenses	($139,000)	($139,000)	($139,000)	($139,000)
Net Pretax Profit (loss)	**$201,000**	**$136,000**	**$26,000**	**($44,000)**
Return on Investment (net profit ÷ expenses)	**145%**	**98%**	**19%**	**−32%**

rate as the property will be owner occupied, but you will get a huge tax break upon sale. As long as you have owned the house and lived in it for two years (legally, two out of the last five years), you can take up to $500,000 ($250,000 if you're single) in profit from the sale income-tax free.

Food for thought: The IRS's two-year rule is not quite as strict as it first appears. Under "hardship" provisions, the homeowner's exemption can be prorated if you must leave your home before two years. That is, you can still expect to get all of your appreciation tax free if you must move because of a job change, health reasons or "unforeseen" circumstances such as a firing, a pay cut or a divorce. As you can see from the spreadsheets, even if you are allowed to take only half of the allowed exemption, in most cases you'd still get all the appreciation.

One big drawback about using the flip house as a primary residence: You have to live there (or look like you do) during the construction. You aren't required to sleep on-site, however, but you should change your voter registration, driver's license and other official documents to the new address. If you are young and hardy, consider moving in as soon as you can; that will save you your own rent money and more firmly establish the new house as your permanent residence. (In any case, because you will have held the property for more than one year, you will be taxed at the lower capital-gains rate, not the regular income rate.)

Now, many property flippers might take issue with this rather high-end example. This San Francisco job is far more extensive and takes far longer than most quick flips do or should. The goal of a typical flipper is to minimize his financial exposure by getting in and out of the flipped property as cheaply and as quickly as possible—for the cost of a low-end kitchen redo, floor refinishing and a paint job all done in the time it takes to close his purchase and his subsequent sale. To do that, you need to focus on distressed or derelict houses that can be acquired well below their renovated value.

But a novice investor competing with experienced flippers

FOOLISH FLIPPING

There is another type of property flipping that is more appropriate to the wildest speculators and quick-money fantasists. The buying and selling of "preconstruction," or "precon," properties has taken hold in resort areas from Florida to Las Vegas to (believe it or not) Bulgaria.

Developers and real-estate brokers encourage property speculators to buy unbuilt condominium units with the implicit promise that the apartments can be sold at a profit later. Of course, the only reason these speculators expect prices will go up is because they believe someone else—retiring baby boomers, Asians and Europeans with lots of cheap dollars or Latin Americans seeking political stability—will come along later and pay more.

There's no better definition of a market mania than "buy now so you can sell when prices go up." That might work for a while or in specific, highly desirable buildings. But as more new buyers get caught up in the mania, the supply of condos will go up, and the overall market grows more risky and unsustainable.

And the speculators end up operating in a market area flooded with new properties, driving down or cooling appreciation in older properties. The result? The owner of last year's hot precon—now a finished, vacant apartment—ends up pricing to compete with this year's hot precon.

In late 2005, advertised prices for virtually identical three-bedroom units in a medium-size, inland complex in the super-hot Fort Lauderdale market varied by just 2 percent—$525,000 for an existing unit and $514,000 for a precon.

❦

and rehabbers is unlikely to find an appropriately down-at-the-heels property, and certainly not in any of today's frothier real-estate markets. So making a substantial profit in a hot market, then, is likely to require a commitment to a higher-quality renovation and, perhaps more important, to a two-year window so as to eliminate any income taxes. (Even Ms. Clark in Rancho Santa Fe still has a chance to see a substantial six-figure profit.)

DUPLEXES AND SMALL APARTMENT HOUSES

A housing market that saw the price of single-family homes skyrocket was not quite so generous to smaller two-family or multifamily properties (two to four units).

Because the universe of home buyers expanded so much in the last 10 years, the universe of renters contracted, and the market for smaller rental properties contracted with them. Think about it: More home buyers means fewer home renters. And fewer renters means less demand for rental properties. Less demand means lower rents. And lower rents mean lower prices. All of which, from an investor's point of view, should be considered a good thing.

Because you can count on all real-estate trends ultimately reversing themselves, smaller-income properties must be considered the closest thing there is to a buyer's market in real estate right now. There are deals out there for investors.

In Memphis, where two-bedroom apartments in better neighborhoods rent from $500 up to $800 a month, good two-family properties can still be bought for far less than a one-bedroom condo on either of the coasts. Memphis is one of those upended markets, where prices don't appreciate that much—the median home price is just $150,000—in large part because there is so much new building there.

But the new homes go up on the metropolitan periphery, while in-town buildings tend to go up in value only modestly. The result? Very attractive opportunities for investors. Recent prices for 40-year-old two-family homes in the 38111 zip code near the University of Memphis main campus, for example, ranged from just $70,000 to $110,000 (yes, you read that right), virtually the same prices as for comparable single-family homes nearby.

CONVERSIONS

One especially lucrative strategy that landlords can take with rental buildings is to convert them into condominiums. Although you are more likely to
see conversions at large multifamily complexes, the process and math work
quite well in even very small buildings—especially in big cities where prices
and demand are high.

And the payoffs can be terrific, since dividing a property always creates
more value. That only makes sense. A landlord grosses more money renting
two 1,000-square-foot apartments than one 2,000-square-foot one. It's true
in sales, too. A house divided stands to make a nice profit.

Consider Steve and Iris's four-unit apartment building in chapter 5, the
$350,000 place in Hoboken throwing off $2,400 a year of predepreciation
income. What would that building be worth if Steve sold the units off individually? Very conservatively, about $1 million. After all, one would be hard-
pressed to find a nice two-bedroom condo anywhere in the greater New York
area for under $400,000, so pricing these at just $250,000 should make for
fairly easy selling.

So if Steve spends $40,000 upgrading each unit and another $40,000
on the rest of the building, the legal process and incidentals, he'd be into
the building for $450,000 (including his original $70,000 down payment and
the $180,000 he's paid on his mortgage) with an additional first-mortgage
balance of about $100,000. Selling the units at $250,000 and spending
$100,000 on sales costs, the landlord-turned-condo-developer makes a pre-
tax profit of about $450,000.

The conversion process is fairly straightforward, although every state
has different laws and procedures. For a good rundown in New York State and
an idea of how it works in general, see the state attorney general's *Coopera-
tive and Condominium Conversion Handbook* (http://www.oag.state.ny.us/
realestate/conversion.html).

You definitely will need your real-estate attorney and contractor to pull
this off, and, depending on your state, you will need an engineer, land sur-
veyor and an architect. Expect to get your banker involved as well. He or she
will need to OK the conversion. And the lender may be able to make a special
financing arrangement for the buyers of your units.

A FIVE-YEAR PLAN FOR A MEMPHIS TWO-FAMILY HOME 1					
Year	**1**	**2**	**3**	**4**	**5**
Rental Income	$12,000	$12,360	$12,731	$13,113	$13,506
Vacancy loss (10%)	($1,200)	($1,236)	($1,273)	($1,311)	($1,351)
Operating expenses	($3,000)	($3,090)	($3,183)	($3,278)	($3,377)
Net operating income	$7,800	$8,034	$8,275	$8,523	$8,779
Mortgage interest	($5,000)	($4,900)	($4,800)	($4,700)	($4,600)
Depreciation	($2,400)	($2,400)	($2,400)	($2,400)	($2,400)
Taxable income	$400	$734	$1,075	$1,423	$1,779
Tax liability @ 33% (savings)	$132	$242	$355	$470	$587
Net operating income	$7,800	$8,034	$8,275	$8,523	$8,779
Annual debt service (principal & interest)	($6,300)	($6,300)	($6,300)	($6,300)	($6,300)
Pretax cash flow	$1,500	$1,734	$1,975	$2,223	$2,479
Tax liability (taxes due)	($132)	($242)	($355)	($470)	($587)
After-Tax Cash Flow	**$1,368**	**$1,492**	**$1,620**	**$1,754**	**$1,892**
Cap rate	6.50%				
Property Value	**$110,000**				**$135,061**
Total Return on Initial Investment of	**$22,000**				**51%**

All of this in an area where you are not likely to see huge price appreciation, which is all the more reason why you want to make sure you operate with a positive cash flow.

So do the math. On paper at least, the two-family homes are a no-brainer. Monthly payments, including insurance and maintenance, on an $88,000 mortgage (20 percent down on the $110,000 property) come to only about $750 a month. So renting both units at the low end of the market would result in a positive after-tax cash flow of more than $100 a month.

And here's what would happen to the same building if you

A FIVE-YEAR PLAN FOR A MEMPHIS TWO-FAMILY HOME 2

Year	1	2	3	4	5
Rental Income	$19,200	$19,776	$20,369	$20,980	$21,610
Vacancy loss (10%)	($1,920)	($1,978)	($2,037)	($2,098)	($2,161)
Operating expenses	($3,000)	($3,090)	($3,183)	($3,278)	($3,377)
Net operating income	$14,280	$14,708	$15,150	$15,604	$16,072
Mortgage interest	($5,000)	($4,900)	($4,800)	($4,700)	($4,600)
Depreciation	($3,490)	($3,490)	($3,490)	($3,490)	($3,490)
Taxable income	$5,790	$6,318	$6,860	$7,414	$7,982
Tax liability @ 33% (savings)	$1,911	$2,085	$2,264	$2,447	$2,634
Net operating income	$14,280	$14,708	$15,150	$15,604	$16,072
Annual debt service (principal & interest)	($6,300)	($6,300)	($6,300)	($6,300)	($6,300)
Pretax cash flow	$7,980	$8,408	$8,850	$9,304	$9,772
Tax liability (taxes due)	($1,911)	($2,085)	($2,264)	($2,447)	($2,634)
After-Tax Cash Flow	**$6,069**	**$6,323**	**$6,586**	**$6,857**	**$7,138**
Cap rate	6.50%				
Property Value	**$110,000**				**$247,266**
Total Return on Initial Investment of	**$52,000**				**227%**

spend an additional $15,000 a unit to upgrade so you can charge top-of-the-market rents of $800 a month.

If you chose to live in one of the units, you could use the other half to significantly reduce your own housing costs. Apply half the annual cash flow to the principal balance on the mortgage, and you will own the place after just 13 years and save $60,000 in interest.

That's Peter Slifirski's plan in New Jersey. He knows a thing or two about real-estate management. He owns a firm that manages 42 condominium buildings. He just built his family a new home, and a big portion of his monthly nut is being paid by the tenants of the rental unit he included in the plans.

It's a four-story town house he built in Hoboken, just across the river from Manhattan, where he and his family live in the top three floors. The tenants pay $2,500 a month to live in a two-bedroom, two-bath first floor rental. It's his fourth rental property.

"Taxes in this town are tremendous," he says, explaining why he built his family's new home with a second unit. "We all want to retire someday and not worry about housing expenses. This is one way to do it."

Good deals on smaller buildings can be found throughout the country, most obviously in cities such as Memphis, Cleveland or Buffalo that have not experienced huge price run-ups. But bargains on smaller income properties can be found even in some of the hottest markets. For example, in trendy Pasadena, California, where even modest homes can sell for $400 to $600 a square foot, two-, three- or four-unit rental buildings can be bought in the $250 to $350 range.

Above this level of buildings, the would-be property maven enters a whole new league, the higher stakes world of commercial real-estate investing. We'll look at that in the next chapter.

CHAPTER 7

GOING COMMERCIAL
LARGER APARTMENT COMPLEXES AND COMMERCIAL BUILDINGS

When we mean to build,
We first survey the plot, then draw the model,
And when we see the figure of the house,
Then must we rate the cost of the erection,
Which if we find outweighs ability,
What do we then but draw anew the model
In fewer offices, or at least desist
To build at all?

—WILLIAM SHAKESPEARE

Going from small residential properties to larger apartment complexes and commercial buildings is like jumping from junior high school straight to college. It's a much different world. Many of the principles are the same, but the costs and potential rewards are exponentially higher.

And, for the moment, out of reach. Most commercial properties require a level of professional management that is beyond the expertise of novice investors. These are not places that a part-time handyman can keep an eye on. These are not properties that a husband and wife can oversee on weekends.

Those are among the lessons learned by New York–based architect-designer Jamie Sowlakis, who stepped into the commercial real-estate business in 1998 with a $2 million project in the tiny, historic village of Litchfield, Connecticut. His main business is high-end residential design and construction.

West Street Yard was a new kind of project for him. The number one lesson?

"We spent more than we thought we would," says Mr. Sowlakis.

He and his partners—an investment banker, an attorney and an interior decorator—brought a considerable array of expertise to the table. But they were unprepared for the minefield of real-estate regulations that even small towns can erect.

The group converted a 2.5-acre, 19th-century lumberyard into an office and retail center that includes a paint store, an upscale spa, a stockbroker's office and a kitchen-cabinet firm. What's not there, however, are a planned restaurant (no way, said the town's zoning board) or prominent signage letting the public know who's doing business in the complex (nixed by the historic preservation committee).

Although Mr. Sowlakis and his partners have managed to maintain 85 percent occupancy and collect rents in the $15-to-$18-per-square-foot range, the project has not been a quick moneymaker for them. They have been fortunate, he says, to have several tenants with long-term leases. That eases the uncertainties that can crop up with a high tenant turnover. Their next step? Convert the entire complex into commercial condominiums—where each office or store is sold off separately.

"This is an exit strategy from a financial standpoint," he says. "It's a way to get our money out."

As Mr. Sowlakis and his partners learned, commercial property investment functions at a number of levels. Operating an existing professional office building is a much different business than developing a new suburban community; building, marketing and managing a high-rise condo project in a newly reborn downtown requires a different set of business skills, contacts and associates than building franchise private-storage facilities in small towns.

Because the novice investor is unlikely to step right into ownership at this level, we will only skim the surface here, looking at some of the main differences about this type of investing and then, as we did in chapter 6, look at some of the specifics of different types of properties.

More to the point, however, we will be looking into the different types of ownership mechanisms that go with commercial investing, the types of financial arrangements and the sets of concerns that you will have as a commercial landlord.

Throughout this chapter, we will be using the term "commercial" to describe all sorts of properties, including larger multifamily residential buildings.

IT'S NOT JUST WHAT YOU OWN, IT'S HOW YOU OWN IT

It is almost always better to own investment properties through some sort of corporate or partnership structure. With smaller buildings, that is rarely for tax purposes, but rather to insulate your personal wealth from lawsuits and other liability issues that can arise. As the financial stakes increase, however, there are more and more compelling reasons to formalize your business within some sort of corporate structure.

There are four types of ownership you will want to consider: sole proprietorships or partnerships, limited partnerships, corporations and limited liability companies. As a rule, your individual liability for the properties' debts declines as you move from one form of ownership to the next.

A **sole proprietorship** is a standard one-person business while a **general partnership** is the typical structure where you and a friend or a spouse go into business together. Both are very easy to set up because you don't need to make any formal structure at all. Your business is you or you and your partner.

On a small-time level, with just one or two properties, there are no real drawbacks to these arrangements. With little debt, some savings and sufficient liability insurance, you are probably safe from excessive claims for unpaid bills, on-site injuries, court judgments or other mishaps.

Important: Each partner is personally liable for the business's debts. And although the partnership can own real estate and other property, both partners will be required to apply for loans, providing their personal financial information with the loan application. And a note of caution: Even though you are not required to, it's always a good idea to have some written agreement between the partners outlining the terms of the partnership. The agreement should also spell out how the partnership will be dissolved should one or both partners decide to call it off.

A **limited partnership** separates the "limited" partners, largely those who put up the capital for a business, from the "general" partner who operates the business. Limited partners are insulated from liability for business debts, but the general partner is not. The general partner alone will be required to file his personal financial information for loans. This form of ownership was quite common among real-estate investors when wealthy individuals bought into limited partnerships because they could write off real-estate losses against other income. That is no longer the case. Today, the limited partner's losses can be written off only against rental income. The legal paperwork with setting up and operating a limited partnership can also be quite expensive and time consuming.

There are two types of corporations: **S corporations,** which are generally small businesses with a limited number of shareholders, and **C corporations,** which are much larger and can have tens of thousands of shareholders. Both require extensive legal work to set up and maintain. Ongoing reporting and corporate governance operations are also cumbersome, especially for C corporations.

S corporations are often a preferred form of ownership for real-estate investors. They operate like a hybrid of a partnership and a corporation inasmuch as they are separate legal entities like corporations, but they pay no corporate income taxes. Profits and losses are passed through to the owners, who then pay only personal income taxes. Real-estate investors seldom operate through C corporations.

Limited liability companies (LLCs) have become quite popular with real-estate investors, as they combine some of the best features of partnerships with corporations. LLC partners, actually called "members," can choose to participate in the management of the business or designate a managing member. But in either case, members, unlike partners, are not individually liable for the LLC's debts. The members can also choose how they are taxed—like a partnership or a C corporation. (Mr. Sowlakis's commercial property is owned by an LLC.)

As your company grows, you may find yourself in a variety of ownership situations. (Remember your network: This is what lawyers and accountants are for.) You may find that you will need to set up multiple corporate layers to handle different properties. For example, the general partner in a limited partnership may actually be an LLC. An S corporation could go into a partnership with an individual or another S corporation to acquire a shopping center, which will be actually owned by a third party that you establish—"S&S Partners," say. Likewise, many properties are owned by a partnership or some other entity, which is itself owned by another.

Landlords are notoriously secretive about their business dealings and often put layer upon layer of ownership entities between themselves and their properties. One relatively recent such ploy has been the use of "land trusts" that put the penultimate level of ownership in the hands of a trustee, and the real—or in this case, "beneficial"—owner's name never shows

FORMS OF REAL-ESTATE OWNERSHIP

	Sole Proprietorship	General Partnership	Limited Partnership
What is it?	One owner; not incorporated.	Two or more owners; both are equally and personally liable for the debts from the business.	Partners conduct a business jointly but are liable only to the extent of the amount of money they have invested; "general partner" operates and has unlimited personal liability.
Suitable for real estate?	Only for investors with very limited property holdings.	Only for limited property holdings.	OK for limited partners; can be costly for the general partner.
Tax treatment	Individual income taxes.	Partners report income and losses on their personal taxes.	Profits are passed through to the limited partners; dividends are exempt from Social Security taxes.
Liability	No protection for personal assets.	No protection for personal assets.	Limited partners protected; general partner isn't.
Pros	No paperwork hassles; simple to set up and operate.	No paperwork hassles; simple to set up and operate.	Investors are protected because their liability is limited to just the capital they invested.
Cons	No asset protection; unlimited personal liability in a lawsuit.	No asset protection; each partner is fully liable.	Expensive to set up and operate.

FORMS OF REAL-ESTATE OWNERSHIP

	C Corporation	S Corporation	Limited Liability Company
What is it?	Legal entity separate and distinct from its shareholder owners; shareholders participate in the profits but are not held personally liable for the company's debts.	"Subchapter S" corporation with a limited number of shareholders; no federal corporate tax, only at the shareholder level.	Corporate-partnership hybrid; shareholders (called "members") have limited liability for the company's actions or debts.
Suitable for real estate?	Preferred for very large operations.	Generally better for individuals engaged in "flipping" properties rather than buying and holding rental buildings.	Preferred method of holding; investors frequently have separate LLCs to own separate properties.
Tax treatment	"Double taxation"; corporation pays taxes on its profits; shareholders are taxed again on dividends. Income shifting between the corporation and the shareholder can, however, reduce overall taxes.	State taxes can vary, but profits are passed through to shareholders; no corporate tax; dividends exempt from Social Security taxes. Shareholders can deduct operating losses.	Tax flexibility; for tax purposes members can choose whether to treat the LLC as a sole proprietorship or a corporation.
Liability	Shareholders have no liability.	Shareholders have no liability.	Members protected, no individual liability.
Pros	Tax-free benefits such as health insurance, retirement plans, tuition programs.	No "double taxation" as profits are passed through. No Social Security taxes on flip income.	Participants can deduct operating losses against regular income; inexpensive to set up and operate.
Cons	Very expensive to set up and maintain.	Limited number of shareholders; no tax-free benefits; expensive to set up and operate.	More flexible than an S corporation, but much more paperwork than proprietorship.

up on a public document. Such arrangements are well beyond the scope of this book.

And in any case, novice investors are unlikely to need a phalanx of corporate constructs to protect their interests in just one, two or a handful of small properties. LLCs work just fine, and many investors set up separate LLCs for each property they own. And it's important to remember that the individual behind the corporate structure is the key player. No one really does business with an unknown company, only people. Especially lenders.

FOLLOW THE MONEY

And borrowing money is how you get in the game. No one this side of the Forbes 400 walks around with enough cash to buy large buildings on his or her own.

The first, big difference between residential and commercial properties comes with how they are financed. Once you pass the four-unit threshold, residential loan rules no longer apply. If you are buying commercial properties, you will be expected to have larger down payments—usually at least 25 percent down on building acquisitions—and shorter loan terms. Interest rates will also be higher. On the plus side, however, you are likely to find lenders far more flexible and creative about commercial loans than they are with residential mortgages. You will find that is especially true for smaller, local banks that operate in the area or neighborhood where you are buying.

Why is that? Because the terms for residential mortgages are for the most part determined by the big, quasi-governmental mortgage backers Fannie Mae and Freddie Mac. That's not the case with commercial loans, where lenders have considerable leeway to structure deals in any legal way that's appropriate. Local banks have a vested interest in lending to local businesses so they can be quite welcoming to property developers and investors in their neighborhoods. Of course, the drawback

FINDING THE MONEY

Commercial lending practices vary by the lender; a good deal for one may not be a good deal for another. Most lenders have minimum and maximum amounts that they will lend on commercial projects. And those can vary by the type of property.

Here are some types of commercial loans and some typical terms.

Fixed-rate and floating-rate. "Conduit" or "CMBS" loans are made by nonbank lenders that pool a number of loans and then package them as "commercial mortgage-backed securities" that are sold in the bond markets. Banks tend to make "portfolio" loans that they keep on their own books. The bigger the lender, the higher the minimum loan. Look for the lowest minimums on multifamily and office buildings. For fixed-rate loans, expect terms up to 20 years with amortization rates up to 30 years. The loan-to-value ratio will be 75 percent. Terms on floating-rate loans will be from one to five years.

Fannie Mae and Freddie Mac. Limited to multifamily properties and senior housing. Terms up to 30 years with 30-year amortization rates. Loan-to-value rates up to 80 percent.

Federal Housing Authority (FHA). Multifamily and health-care properties with terms up to 40 years for new projects. The maximum loan-to-value on apartment buildings is 85 percent.

Interim or bridge. Usually adjustable-rate loans that run from 6 to 36 months. Loan-to-value rates will be in the 75 percent to 80 percent range.

Mezzanine. Mezzanine loans are similar to second mortgages, but they are secured by the stock of the company that owns the property, as opposed to the real estate itself. That gives the lender considerable leeway should the loan go into default. The lender can foreclose on the stock in a matter of a few weeks, as opposed to the months or years it can take to foreclose a mortgage. Terms will vary with the lender and the deal.

to going to a smaller bank is it is *small.* Don't expect a bank with just $100 million dollars in assets to bankroll a $50 million project. But a $1 million strip mall with an anchor tenant already onboard is just the kind of deal any local banker dreams of making.

Don't forget your business plan. As with all lending, your loan application will be approved if you can pay the money back. If you can confidently show that your real-estate business can make the loan payments along with its other obligations, then any lender will be predisposed to doing a deal with you.

REMEMBER, IT'S A BUSINESS

Everything we have said throughout this book about real-estate investing as a business goes triple in the commercial world.

While profit margins in commercial real estate can soar, the margins for error are much narrower than in the small residential world. And your responsibilities as the owner-manager of a commercial property are far more serious. Your tenants will not look kindly on anything that goes on at the building that interferes with their own businesses. Their livelihoods will depend on their offices or stores being open and operating properly. They pay good money for good service. They will expect the electricity to always be on, the water to always flow, the heat and air-conditioning to always work, the elevators to always function and all the public areas and grounds and the parking lots to always look their best. And whenever problems arise, they will expect them to be fixed immediately. Or sooner.

That's why the owners of most commercial properties rely on professional managers to oversee their buildings. While some large, integrated real-estate companies do everything— develop, build, market and manage—most owners are ill-equipped to perform all the necessary day-to-day operations.

One area that owners should take primary responsibility for, however, is leasing. Leases are the real assets of any investment property because they determine just how much money the property makes and, therefore, what the property is worth. Yes, the building is the primary asset, but it makes no money on its own. It has to have people living in it or operating businesses

RENTAL TERMS

Commercial leases come in two basic types: "gross" and "net." Generally, you will find variations of gross leases in residential and office buildings; net leases are more prevalent in retail and industrial properties. That is changing, however, and more and more office leases are being written as net leases.

Local customs can vary, but gross leases usually require the landlord to pay some or all of a building's or unit's operating expenses, such as utilities, insurance and maintenance.

Under net leases, however, tenants pay "additional rent" to cover those costs—over and above the rent they pay for the space they occupy. You will often see these referred to as "NNN" (net-net-net) leases. NNN leases started out in industrial properties, where one tenant occupied a building. The thinking behind these leases was that all the operating costs of the building were for the benefit of the one tenant, who should therefore pay for them.

From a landlord's point of view, NNN leases are clearly a good deal as they assure that rents will go up with the costs of operation. You won't be caught holding the bag if heating oil spikes or electric rates suddenly take off. Today, NNN leases are also often viewed as advantageous to tenants as well, as they have more flexibility controlling some of their costs.

Another type of lease you may encounter in retail properties is the "percentage lease," which calls for the landlord to be paid a percentage of the tenant's gross. There is usually a base rent amount to which a percentage rent is then added.

from it if it is to have any ongoing value as an investment. That's where leases come in, and where you as the owner should invest your time and energy.

Residential leases usually run for no more than a year or two and outline the basic terms of the tenancy—set regular rent increases while outlining the obligations of the tenant and the landlord. The owners of larger residential properties will have leases written especially for them, while a typical landlord of medium-size apartment buildings (less than 50 units) is quite likely to use a lease form bought at a stationery store or downloaded from the Web.

But a commercial lease is an art form, and negotiating it is too important for anyone to take charge of but the building owner. That's you.

While there are plenty of circumstances that allow for standardized lease arrangements, you should plan on having your own standard lease (but leave the writing to your lawyer). And you should consider most of it nonnegotiable. But be prepared to haggle over some points. Every business operator sees his or her situation as unique. They, like you, are obligated to minimize their expenses, and rent is one of the biggest expenses that any business faces.

MULTIFAMILY BUILDINGS AND COMPLEXES

Your first foray in the commercial realm will most likely come with an opportunity to acquire a larger, multifamily apartment house. It's a big step, whether you move up to just a six- or eight-unit building or a small complex with 15 to 25 apartments. At these sizes you can probably still handle all the management chores yourself. But as you acquire more and larger buildings with more tenants and more need for daily attention, you will definitely need more professional help.

That will come first in the need for a full-time supervisor—aka a "super"—whether to oversee the day-to-day maintenance and upkeep issues at one large building or several smaller ones. (Remember: You want to acquire properties that are all close to each other. One super can handle multiple buildings if they are nearby.) Depending on local practices, you may be expected to provide your full-time super with an apartment, along with an appropriate salary and benefits.

A good super is more than worth the cost. He or she will not only handle routine maintenance matters—the clogged drain in apartment 12B—but you can also rely on the super to see that tenant move-ins and move-outs are handled without too much damage to the building, to clean and prepare vacant apartments for rental, to make sure that the garbage is getting picked up and trash isn't strewn around the property, to shovel snow from sidewalks, and any of a host of other daily duties that you as the owner don't want to deal with.

Supers are so valuable that where I live in New York City, they can make six-figure incomes at large buildings. Depending on the size of the property, the super might oversee a substantial staff; a 300-unit complex easily could require a permanent full-time staff of two dozen or more people. And supers usually stay with buildings even as owners come and go.

Next up the staff ladder is a resident manager. Just as the super's job is to tend to the building, the resident manager's job is to tend to the tenants—collect rents, see that building rules are followed, handle complaints, collect applications from prospective tenants and show vacant apartments.

Like a good super, a good resident manager is well worth the pay. At the least, it's a full-time second set of eyes and ears on the premises. Only at the largest buildings and complexes, however, must you consider the resident manager a full-time job. Toward the lower range of buildings, in fact, it is quite common for the resident manager to be just a longtime tenant who performs the manager duties in exchange for a reduced rent. (Warning: The IRS could interpret a rent reduction as taxable compensation. And you could be required to pay Social Security and Medicare taxes as well.)

Sometimes the wife or husband of the super may perform the duties of a resident manager. Obviously, the bigger the building, the more that will be required of a resident manager, and the more likely that you will need to hire someone on a part- or full-time basis.

Eventually, a resident manager will not suffice. As your real-estate empire grows, you will need a management company or your own full-time staff of managers and salespeople.

Rule of thumb: As your real-estate empire approaches the 100-unit threshold, expect employee costs to become a significant line item—10 percent to 15 percent of your gross rental revenues.

OFFICE BUILDINGS

If you want to know what you need to know about office buildings, start with two books. Neither of them has anything to do with the dollars-and-cents issues facing novice real-estate investors, but both have everything to do with how this, the roughest part of the real-estate business, operates. The higher the stakes, the less idealistic the players. You're a bright person. You'll learn the right lessons.

Empire: A Tale of Obsession, Betrayal, and the Battle for an American Icon (Wiley), by my *Wall Street Journal* colleague Mitchell Pacelle, tells the remarkable story of how the late real-estate magnate Harry Helmsley (husband of the convicted tax evader Leona Helmsley), a disgraced Japanese businessman and Donald Trump jockeyed for control of the 102-story Empire State Building. You just don't get better actors than this.

A history of the world's most famous office building, Mr. Pacelle's soap opera of intrigue and double dealing is far too rich and its story too convoluted to go into here with much detail. In a nutshell, it tells how Mr. Trump gained control of the building from Hideki Yokoi, but ultimately lost out on operating it when he was unable to break a 114-year master lease held by the Helmsley interests. Favorite anecdote: A tenant's secretary, hoping to help Mr. Trump take control, collected dead mice to try to demonstrate that the Helmsleys weren't maintaining the building under the terms of the lease.

Later, after the book's conclusion, Helmsley ally Peter Malkin bought the 102-story landmark in 2002 for only $57 million dollars—just a few million more than media mogul Rupert Murdoch and his wife recently paid for a Fifth Avenue co-op apartment once owned by a Rockefeller. (Food for thought: Which tycoon do you suppose made the better real-estate investment?)

Less entertaining but no less insightful, the other book to read is *Form Follows Finance* (Princeton Architectural Press), by Carol Willis, founder and director of the Skyscraper Museum in New York. She shows how the design of modern office buildings results mainly from the economics of real-estate development and not from the fashion whims of the latest, hottest architects. American cities, Ms. Willis asserts, are built by businessmen, not artists.

Mundane considerations such as the need for air circulation and natural light in buildings built before World War II dictated how the first great generation of office buildings was designed. Ms. Willis contrasts early 20th-century building practices in Chicago and New York to demonstrate that the look of the modern skyline is mostly the result of how developers respond to rental-market considerations, local regulations, zoning and, most important, the street grid.

The two cities' differing architectural styles were mainly the result of owners and architects following the fundamental dictate of development: Buildings are what you need to make the land pay for itself.

In Chicago, builders erected giant, block-sized office buildings mainly because that was how the city was laid out in the 19th century—in large, square blocks bounded by wide avenues. Buildings featured massive footprints with open cores for ventilation and light. As a result, Chicago skyscrapers boasted considerable square footage but rarely reached the dizzying heights of the towers of lower Manhattan. There, in contrast, a maze of narrow 17th- and 18th-century streets forced builders to go tall and slender, and regulations required higher floors to be set back from the street. So the skyscrapers of downtown New York look much different than those of the Chicago Loop, even though they were built at the same time.

Take Ms. Willis's observations into the current building environment and you can see how the Interstate Highway System encouraged the building of modern office parks and corporate campuses sprawling across hundreds of acres of inexpensive suburban land, or why local governments, desperate to maintain their downtown tax bases, encouraged developers to refashion city street grids, raze multiple blocks of older, smaller buildings and erect giant, self-contained mega-structures such as the Renaissance Center in Detroit, the Bunker Hill development in Los Angeles or the destroyed World Trade Center in New York.

Enough with the history lesson. As an investor, your interests are not that different in a commercial building than in a typical multifamily residential building: You want to keep good, paying tenants by providing them good service. That means you will need full-time staff to handle maintenance and property upkeep.

Office buildings, whether situated downtown or in a suburb come in three general types: "Class A," "Class B" or "Class C" properties. You can have low-rise Class A buildings and high-rise Class Cs. It all depends on the condition of the property, the tenants and the neighborhood. You know them when you see them.

Newer, landmark-style buildings that house big, well-known companies, leading law firms or other topflight tenants are typically considered Class A. They are in the most desirable parts of town, have the most up-to-date features and amenities and command the highest rents. Class A buildings can house one company or many, but they frequently have one tenant who has paid for the property's naming or signage rights. It may be called the XYZ Tower even though that company may occupy only a few of the floors.

In cities that have experienced significant rehabilitation of older neighborhoods, the distinctions between Class A buildings and others may be less than obvious. Design firms and advertising agencies pay rents for converted warehouse spaces in San Francisco's once gritty SoMa (South of Market) neighborhood that rival any in the city's high-rise financial district.

GOOD RETURNS

Few novice investors will start very high up the office-building food chain. Far more likely will be the opportunity to acquire much more modest buildings, such as a "professional" office building occupied by a number of doctors' and dentists' offices and other health-care industry operations. Every city has such buildings. Your own doctor's office is probably in one.

In fact, many physicians and other high-revenue producers have become landlords themselves, acquiring properties large enough for their own operations and others'. Sales and rental prices are all over the map, so there are few hard-and-fast rules that apply across the country.

Still, it is standard that office rents are expressed as an annual cost per-square-foot price. So 1,500 square feet of typical Class B medical-office space in the Dallas area, for example, rents in the $18- to $22-per-square-foot range, while buildings with up to 30,000 square feet of rentable space can be bought for less than $80 a square foot. As you can see, the raw numbers suggest a good possible return for a relatively modest investment:

Purchase price	($80/sq. ft.)	$2,400,000
Down payment	25.0%	$600,000
Amount financed		$1,800,000
Rental revenue	($20/sq. ft)	$600,000
Operating expenses	(45% of revs)	$270,000
Mortgage payment	6.5%	$136,800
Gross Profit		**$193,200**

Class B buildings are usually older and not so on the cutting edge of design or amenities. They remain highly desirable, however, for many tenants because they are usually in or very near preferred business districts. They also offer landlords considerable opportunity for upgrading and raising

COMPARING PROPERTIES

BOMA International, the Building Owners and Managers Trade Association, categorizes office buildings into three classes. Here's what the group says.

"These classes represent a subjective quality rating of buildings which indicates the competitive ability of each building to attract similar types of tenants. A combination of factors including rent, building finishes, system standards and efficiency, building amenities, location/accessibility and market perception is used as relative measures. . . ."

Class A: "Most prestigious buildings competing for premier office users with rents above average for the area. Buildings have high quality standard finishes, state-of-the-art systems, exceptional accessibility and a definite market presence."

Class B: "Buildings competing for a wide range of users with rents in the average range for the area. Building finishes are fair to good for the area and systems are adequate, but the building does not compete with Class A at the same price."

Class C: "Buildings competing for tenants requiring functional space at rents below the average for the area."

Sources: BOMA International; photos by Gary Leonard, Los Angeles

rents, as many Class B buildings can be renovated and modernized back into Class A properties.

Class C buildings are more problematic. Generally much older, Class C buildings are usually in marginal—or worse—neighborhoods. They are obsolete and undesirable for most top tenants. Rents are low and many of the existing tenants may be marginal themselves. Consequently, Class C buildings get the lowest rents, have high vacancy rates and minimal services.

Such buildings can be saved. But that usually means rehabilitation of the entire neighborhood, an undertaking that requires tremendous combined efforts by local governments and private companies. If that happens, older buildings often are converted to mixed uses, such as retail or services on the ground floor and offices or apartments on the upper floors. The returns to investors in such areas can be fantastic, but the process can be daunting to even experienced developers.

RETAIL PROPERTIES

Like other types of commercial properties, all but the smallest of retail centers are beyond the financial reach and managerial expertise of novice investors. Depending on its location, a major "power center" featuring an array of big-box retailers such as Wal-Mart or Home Depot can easily be worth $100 million or more. And big, regional shopping malls with a mix of major department stores, smaller national boutique chains, restaurants and other services can cost two or three times that to develop and build.

New commercial investors interested in retail properties will need to focus on small "strip" shopping centers and slightly larger "neighborhood" centers, such as Mr. Sowlakis's complex in Connecticut. Given the high rate of failure among new small businesses, however, such properties are often a mixed bag. There will be ample opportunities to suffer prolonged vacancies, but the returns can be substantial. As most retailers have NNN (net) leases, the landlord's day-to-day expenses can be quite manageable. The gold mine in these kinds of properties comes in landing a secure long-term tenant or two.

Look around. The best, most successful strip centers—5,000 to 20,000 square-foot operations that can be found in both dense urban areas and the most distant exurbs—include at least one major tenant. You want a recognizable convenience store or a national food chain that doesn't always rely on standalone buildings. The minimum size for a 7-Eleven store, for instance, is just 1,200 square feet; 1,500 for a Dunkin' Donuts. Such "mini-anchor" businesses often share shopping-center space with more local businesses such as coin-operated laundries, hair salons, shoe-repair shops or noncompeting mom-and-pop restaurants. (Mr. Sowlakis's West Street Yard is 30,000 square feet in all with one larger anchor tenant and some smaller retailers.)

Even without a national anchor, strip centers can offer nice investing opportunities, especially if the surrounding neighborhood remains healthy and if you remain selective about your tenants. Don't rent to a pawnshop or a liquor store unless you want their customers on your property. Attract tenants who will attract the kinds of people you want frequenting your building.

Prices can range all over the map, depending on the tenants. Typical well-maintained properties in good areas in larger metropolitan areas should run in the $100- to $150-per-square-foot range. But be prepared for sticker shock if you are looking at especially attractive buildings; prices well above $200 a square foot are hardly unknown. Typical annual rents will run from about $25 to $35 a square foot. But be prepared for a nice windfall if your property is in a particularly tony retail area. Rents on the local equivalent of Rodeo Drive or Madison Avenue can easily triple rents on comparable retail buildings elsewhere in town.

A step up the retail food chain are the 50,000-square-foot-plus neighborhood centers that are usually anchored by a major supermarket or drugstore, or both, and may feature some smaller stores as well. Such major tenants rarely move or shut down, so the value of the property is determined in large part by their presence. As a result, the properties can be easier to sell than centers that don't have big, well-known names attached to them.

Although the buildings are much larger than strip centers and the overall prices much greater, per-square-foot figures are usually lower, well below $100 and frequently in the $50 to $70 range. Rents should run from $15 to $20.

MIXED-USE PROPERTIES

The real-estate market in New York City is hardly indicative of the rest of the country. But it's worth noting here that two of the city's newest major developments are giant mixed-use properties staring at each other across Central Park. On the West Side, at Columbus Circle (59th Street and 8th Avenue), stands the new, twin-towered $1.7 billion Time Warner Center. It encompasses the headquarters of the world's largest media company, multimillion-dollar condominiums, a $600-a-night hotel, a high-end shopping mall, a collection of the city's most expensive restaurants, a new performance hall for Lincoln Center, a parking garage and the city's largest supermarket.

Directly across town, at 58th and Lexington, stands the $450 million Bloomberg Tower, headquarters of another media company, along with more than 100 condominiums, more upscale shopping, and Manhattan's first Home Depot (with doormen, no less).

Both properties reflect a wave of major mixed-use development that has been transforming cities and suburbs since the early 1990s. Today, just about every major metropolitan area boasts similarly large-scaled retail-office-residential hybrids: Atlanta, Denver, Fort Worth, San Jose, Charlotte and St. Petersburg, to name a few.

Birkdale Village, for example, is a 52-acre mixed-use development located in Huntersville, North Carolina, near Charlotte.

The project features a Main Street with a typical suburban mix of nearly 300,000 square feet of office and retail (Ann Taylor Loft to Williams-Sonoma) and more than 300 "urban-style" apartments with rents ranging from $900 a month for a one-bedroom "loft efficiency" to $2,200 for a three-bedroom, two-bath town house.

Across the country, Santana Row is an entirely new "European" neighborhood built in 2002 on the site of a former open-air market in San Jose, California. The site features half a million square feet of retail topped with condos, rental apartments and a 200-room hotel.

Of course, the finances and logistics of such projects dwarf the resources and abilities of novice investors. But much smaller mixed-use projects are becoming permanent fixtures in rehabilitated inner-city neighborhoods and in older, close-in suburbs. Most notably, mixed-use properties are the dominant building type in older neighborhoods that have become fashionable. The loft-style apartment building with *the* hot new restaurant or chic boutique on the first floor has become a fixture in most cities. Architects, designers and other creative professionals feel far more comfortable working or living in hip, mixed neighborhoods than in suburban office parks or downtown high-rises.

From the investor's point of view, the finances for smaller mixed-use buildings should be no more daunting than for any other property. As with all rehab projects, however, be aware that you are not in a position to turn around or change an entire neighborhood, just your building. You don't want to be all alone in a neighborhood that is not generally improving.

INDUSTRIAL PROPERTIES

Like office buildings, industrial properties can vary greatly in price and quality, though the issue of neighborhood desirability may not be quite so strong. Heavy industries—think steel, industrial machines, chemicals—tend to congregate in older, grittier industrial areas, usually, but not always, in the cities and mill towns of the Northeast and Midwest.

Lighter industries—high-tech manufacturers, software firms and distribution centers—have grown up mostly in the Sunbelt, where land and labor have both been historically cheaper and local governments have been more welcoming with tax givebacks and other employment incentives.

Most industrial properties are now relegated to large privately owned industrial parks that might share some space with office buildings and a few retail establishments, such as restaurants and banks, catering to the workforce.

Although the finances of big parks are daunting, the costs of individual industrial buildings can be quite reasonable. Good stand-alone properties in the 25,000- to 50,000-square-foot range can be bought in the Sunbelt for as little as $50 a square foot (NNN leases are common at $10 a square foot or less), while marginal properties can be bought for per-square-foot prices in the teens.

The big concern you want to have is too much reliance on a single tenant. Manufacturing can be fickle; factories humming at full capacity in the spring can be shut permanently in the fall when a contract expires or consumer preferences change. Better to have a mix of tenants in different industries, either in one larger building or in a collection of smaller ones.

LAND

Legend has it that the late Sam Walton, founder of Wal-Mart, used to fly over towns he was considering for new stores just so he could get an eagle's eye view of which way the place was growing. Where he saw new houses, new businesses, new roads and highways is where he would build his new store.

Good lesson: If you are going to make money buying and selling land, make sure it's where people are headed.

There are two basic ways to make money on raw land: You can "bank" it or you can develop it.

LAND USE

Zoning issues—what you can legally do with a particular piece of property—invariably play a big part in commercial real-estate investing. Zoning matters are unique to towns and cities, so the mind-numbing classifications will differ from place to place. But you will need to know about the various uses that local governments allow and where. As an example, here is a much simplified breakdown of the zoning districts in just one medium-size city, Tucson, Arizona.

OS Open Space. Used for protection of permanent open space.

IR Institutional Reserve. Federal, state, city, county and other properties under public ownership, which are natural reserves or wildlife refuge reserves.

RH Rural Homestead. Primarily low-density residential property, with limited commercial and industrial uses to service residential development.

SR, RX-1, RX-2 Low-Density Residential. Primarily low-density residential property, with recreational/tourist-related enterprises permitted subject to lot size.

R-1 Residential—Single-Family. Primarily for the use of single-family residences. Schools, churches and public buildings permitted.

R-2 Medium-Density Residential. Multifamily and single-family residences permitted.

R-3 High-Density Residential. Primarily for apartment houses; single-family development permitted.

MH-2 Mobile Home Park. Mobile-home parks or mobile-home subdivisions, along with social, commercial and recreation facilities permitted as secondary uses.

O-1, O-2 Low-Intensity Office. Allows for conversion of residential to office use, primarily for properties located on arterial and/or collector streets.

O-3 Office. Professional and semiprofessional office, high-density residential developments and limited research and development uses permitted.

NC Neighborhood Commercial. Low-intensity, small-scale commercial and office uses that are compatible in size and design with adjacent residential uses.

C-1 Local Commercial. A restrictive commercial zone, limited to retail sales with no outside display/storage. Office and residential development permitted. Restaurants permitted.

C-2, C-3 General and Intensive Commercial. Retail commercial with wholesale; nightclubs, bars, amusement enterprises permitted. Full range of automotive activities; sales, repair, leasing, etc. Limited manufacturing permitted. Residential uses permitted.

P Parking. Off-street parking at or below grade.

OCR-1, OCR-2 Office/Commercial/Residential. High-rise mixed office, commercial and residential uses located in major activity centers.

MU Multiple Use. A mixed-use zone permitting low- to medium-density residential development and various commercial activities commonly from the O-3 to C-2 zones.

P-I Park Industrial. The most restrictive of industrial zones. Administrative, manufacturing and wholesale activities carried on entirely within an enclosed structure. Limited retail sales permitted when incidental to an industrial use.

I-1, I-2 Light and Heavy Industrial. Commercial, industrial and manufacturing uses; residential restricted to caretakers residence, except for Resident Artisans in the Downtown Warehouse District.

Source: City of Tucson, Summary of Zoning Classifications and Development Designators, *2001*

Banking is the "buy-and-hold" of a parcel that you believe will become more valuable at some point in the future. On the mega-deal scale, land banking is quite the norm in Las Vegas, where hotel and gaming companies buy, hold and trade bare desert parcels like kids swapping baseball cards. At the center of the giant $7.9 billion acquisition of Mandalay Resorts by MGM Mirage that closed in 2005, for example, were 100 acres of undeveloped land on the fabled Las Vegas Strip. The four parcels were valued for tax purposes at $24 million per acre, a third of the value of a deal that included four brand-name hotel-casinos. But here's the kicker: Just 10 years earlier, Mandalay had acquired the biggest portion of that undeveloped land for just $1 million an acre.

"We all should have bought property back in 1977," MGM chairman Terry Lanni told the *Las Vegas Review-Journal* at the time that the deal was announced. "We could have just taken a dart gun and [picked] anywhere and done well with it."

On a more down-to-earth level, smaller investors can bank properties, too, either buying and holding larger parcels in the path of development or picking up "remnant" lots in developing or already developed areas. You can find these remnant lots in even the best newer neighborhoods or subdivisions. By definition, every place has some properties that are less desirable than others—landlocked lots in a lake community, for example, or residential-zoned parcels that front on major streets.

You can count on the original developers of the subdivision to try to hold on to these parcels for only a short while and then to sell them at a steep discount. They are not in the land-banking business; they are in the land-developing business and are eager to move on to the next project. If the neighborhood is a good one, and if you are patient, you may eventually be able to sell a remnant lot at a profit. Your carrying costs will be low—taxes, and perhaps some owners' association fees—but you will have no depreciation since you are not allowed to depreciate land.

Land banking tends to work better in commercially zoned areas because it's easier to make the land pay for itself while you wait for the value to increase. Quite common in commercial areas are parking lots or inexpensive "tax-payer" buildings that produce a bit of income, but not as much as the full potential of the property. In a city neighborhood, a tax-payer might be a parking lot or a one- or two-story building with a nonchain fast-food restaurant or a mom-and-pop store surrounded by high-rise offices and apartment buildings. On the suburban fringe, a tax-payer may be a small strip center that takes up just a portion of a larger parcel.

It's a short step from building a tax-payer to becoming a developer. And that is where the real money is when it comes to land investing. You will need at least an acre for a typical suburban strip center (one acre equals 43,560 square feet), two-thirds of which will end up as parking space.

There are two types of improvements that you, the developer, can make to a piece of raw land: hard and soft improvements, aka "tangible" and "intangible." Hard improvements, as the name suggests, involve bringing utilities to the site, as well as grading and paving, building and any other permanent changes to the property. Soft improvements are zoning changes, planning approvals and financing—even architectural drawings.

Don't go trying to develop a parcel in the middle of nowhere or build an industrial park in the middle of a residential neighborhood. But in the right, desirable area, most improved properties will be relatively easy to sell at a good profit.

Warning: With no track record, you are most unlikely to get a bank loan on raw land that you plan to bank. You'll have to rely on loans against other income properties, personal assets or, as a last resort, unsecured loans such as credit cards.

Marc Asselin, a land trader in Florida, and his partners buy lots in the $20,000–$30,000 range and then resell them in the hot local market. They got started in business by pooling money they'd raised from home-equity lines of credit on their personal residences, although now he says they have enough money in the bank that they hardly need to use the credit lines.

You can get development loans, however. But you will be expected to have a substantial interest in the land, which you may then be required to put up for collateral. Also expect the lender who is funding your development project to require that any outstanding loan on the land be paid off or made "subordinate" so that the maker of the loan on the raw land is in a secondary position.

Generally, commercial real estate is usually a far better business than residential because it is more predictable. Outside so-called trophy properties (think of the story of the Empire State Building), expect the commercial market to be far less speculative as more professionals are involved and values are more tightly tied to income production.

Still, even experienced property magnates can get carried away. That's why you might want to stop and reflect for a moment before you make the leap into real-estate investing. In the next chapter, we ask the question that all potential Donald Trumps should ask.

CHAPTER 8

DO YOU REALLY WANT TO BE A LANDLORD?

If property had simply pleasures, we could stand it; but its duties make it unbearable.

— OSCAR WILDE

A landlord is someone everyone loves to hate. From the top-hatted, mustachioed baddies of silent movies to the *Village Voice*'s annual "worst landlords" lists, the public has long enjoyed reviling property owners. Everyone has a story about a lousy landlord.

But landlords, too, have plenty of stories. Spend an evening with a group of owners or visit the discussion forums at landlord.com (http://www.landlord.com), and the tales will astound you. There's the landlord scared out of his wits by the drug dealer operating out of the rented apartment. How about the tenant who locked the landlord out, removed the

DID YOU HEAR ABOUT THE TENANT...?

Landlords' comments posted in the discussion forums of landlord.com:

"I had a tenant move out last month after two years paying on time every time. She left no new address and an ugly problem. Almost every day, men come knock on the doors, knock on the windows and stop the new tenant to ask for 'girls.' Now I guess what business the former tenant ran inside my rental property. I think two years of clients will take a while to get rid of."

"I recently had a very friendly tenant with whom I had a 'verbal' lease only to find out later his hobby is growing and selling marijuana from my apartment!! It is amazing how powerless I felt, and I'm an owner-occupied landlord. He eventually moved out after using his security deposit as last month's rent and putting his fist through my ceiling in a few places. I don't dare sue him for damages because I don't want to find a brick through my window and other vandalism."

"We purchased a repossessed home where the previous owners left several animals. The animals did a good deal of damage and starved to death. Now it's a cleanup issue. Carpet has been removed and all surfaces washed down . . . and the smell remains. Is this a do-it-yourself issue or are professionals the only way?"

"My tenants signed a one-year lease, but after the first month they started pushing the rent day later and later. Now, they owe me about two months' rent, and they probably will not pay. I want to evict them, but there are three families in my house, including my family. My family is living in the basement. But it's against the law, and I am afraid that the tenants will sue me for this if I sue them for eviction."

"Landlord A: I had a tenant who stole my sofa bed, refrigerator, dresser, TV and microwave. I called the police and made a report. A couple of days later I found out they were arrested while staying at my place for stealing from an apartment complex they stayed before renting from me. And yes, it was a refrigerator."

"Landlord B: I had a tenant take the kitchen cabinets once."

"I have a tenant who has three other adults living in the house who are not on the lease. Plus, she's three months behind on her rent. I would like to evict her and take my house back. The tenant said the people don't live there, but every time I go to make a repair I see the people in the beds or walking through the house in pajamas."

fire alarms and then complained to the fire inspector that the apartment had no alarms and the landlord wouldn't come to install them?

Consider yourself warned: Whatever outrageous thing can happen in a rented property will happen. You must steel yourself for this eventuality. If you are not constitutionally suited for this kind of work—for that's what it is—then you probably shouldn't get involved with direct property ownership.

In this chapter, we will cover some of the finer points of landlording, laying out some management tips and looking at what you can and cannot do as a property owner renting to tenants. We will explore practical matters as well as legal ones. As throughout the book, we're concentrating on the owners of smaller properties, since those are where novice real-estate investors are most likely to get started.

While you can hire people to unclog toilets, shovel snow, repaint apartments, even screen new tenants, those people will cost you money, and that money will come out of your profits.

More important, however, a manager who is unfamiliar with all the operations of his or her business is not much of a manager. He's a patsy, a mark, like a befuddled car owner at the mercy of a mechanic. A landlord who doesn't intimately know how his buildings operate is just waiting to be taken on a costly ride. That is not to say that you should always plan on doing all the work yourself, only that you should familiarize yourself with what needs to be done.

As a landlord, you should know, for example, that you don't have to pay to replace a clogged showerhead when all that's really necessary is to flush out the filter of the one that's there. You should know that your tenant's lease specifically prohibits another person moving in without notice and without paying a rent increase. You should know that your contract with the fuel company calls for the furnace to be inspected and serviced every fall. If you delegate all of these matters to others and don't follow what is going on, you run the risk of losing touch with your property and being taken advantage of by contractors, tenants and even your own employees.

This chapter is not exhaustive. You will need to consult specialized property-management guides, the best of which are *Landlording,* by Leigh Robinson (ExPress Publishing), now in its ninth edition, and *Every Landlord's Legal Guide,* by Marcia Stewart, Ralph Warner and Janet Portman (Nolo Press). These are both excellent general guides, and both include plenty of sample forms (tenant applications, reference checks, leases and rental agreements, etc.) that you may copy for your own use.

Be aware, however, that legal issues regarding housing vary greatly from state to state. The Nolo Press maintains links to state housing laws at www.nolo.com, but that is no substitute for your own local lawyer.

INSURANCE

A landlord needs insurance, and plenty of it. As property owners in New Orleans can attest, disasters happen. And you don't have to have levees collapse underneath a Category 5 hurricane just to be ruined. Calamities, natural and man-made, can happen anywhere, any time.

Expect insurance costs to run about 2 percent to 2.5 percent of your annual gross, according to the National Apartment Association.

Residential property owners should carry multiple types of insurance.

- **General property coverage.** Often called "property and casualty" insurance, this is most like typical homeowners' insurance and covers damage to the building from fire, storm or other incidents. It does not cover the loss of tenants' property, however. Be sure your policy includes "rental value insurance," which compensates you for lost rental and other income in addition to your property loss. (Good business practice: You can require that tenants have renters' insurance as a term of the lease. You might even be able to work out an arrangement with an insurer to include coverage in the rent and make a little extra profit as well.)

- **Specialized property coverage.** Insurers love to split hairs when it comes to paying off: "Was that the water or the wind that swept your building across the highway?" Flood insurance is specific coverage that should compensate you for water-related damage and loss resulting from natural or man-made disasters. Watch closely for the definition of "inundation," which should cover mud flows (attention, owners of California canyon properties) as well as the more obvious types of flooding. The federal government administers the National Flood Insurance Program, and insurance companies issue the policies. Specialized coverage is common wherever particular risks are greatest. Californians should have separate earthquake insurance. Properties in the coastal sections of Texas require special windstorm coverage, while policies written in the Pacific Northwest frequently include special volcano clauses.

- **Liability coverage.** This is important. General liability insurance is what protects you when your tenant trips over his own kid's tricycle on your walkway and then sues you for not maintaining a safe environment. Typical coverage should include bodily injury, property damage, personal injury and damage from slander or false advertising. (The last can be more common than you might imagine, especially if your resident manager has a habit of talking to tenants about their neighbors.) It's difficult to put a dollar figure on how much coverage you should have, but in today's litigious world $1 million is not unheard of for owners of even small properties. That's why you should complement your general policy with a relatively inexpensive "umbrella" policy covering extraordinary claims. Otherwise, you will be responsible for any damages over the dollar limit of your general policy. One more thing: If you use your personal automobile to visit your properties, be sure that it is included in your business liability coverage.

If all of this insurance talk is a bit mind numbing, there's a reason that an independent insurance agent (one who does not work for just one company) and an independent adjuster are good candidates for your extended network of real-estate professionals. You'll need the agent when you get ready to close your deal on a property, as no lender is going to fund a loan on an uninsured building.

Most people are familiar with insurance agents and have a good grasp on what they do. But an adjuster is someone you may never meet and may never even need. But, if you do, you'll be glad you have your own—a so-called public adjuster—and not one who works for the insurance company. Insurance companies love to boast in their advertising how quickly they get their adjusters to the scene of a tragedy—some homeowners were being visited in southern Louisiana the morning after Hurricane Katrina hit. The welcome image of the insurance company on the scene, checkbook in hand, is a comforting one. But it's also misleading. Property owners who take early insurance company settlement offers are probably not getting their full due.

When you think about it, the value of hiring a public adjuster is obvious. A public adjuster works for the landlord. He reviews the terms of the insurance coverage, represents the property owner's interest in negotiations with the insurance company's claims experts and is paid with a percentage of an insurance settlement. An insurance company adjuster is paid, well, by the insurance company. So who's going to fight harder to see that the replacement clause in the contract means the insurance company will pay enough to actually rebuild the burned-out building?

CHOOSING TENANTS

As you know, you can't refuse to rent to people because of race, religion, national origin, age, family status, disabilities, gender, sources of income, marital status or sexual orientation.

So get over it. No one's infringing on your rights as a property owner.

However, equal-opportunity laws don't force you to rent to anyone who comes along. The law prevents you only from *not renting* to someone you don't like for the wrong reasons. There's still ample opportunity to exercise your judgment and to make reasoned decisions regarding with whom you wish to do business.

So how do you select tenants, and what sort of criteria are you legally allowed to consider?

The most important criteria are a prospective tenant's finances and rental history. You want a tenant with the resources to pay all the up-front rental costs, the monthly rent, other necessary housing costs and any additional living expenses. You also want a person who has been a good tenant in his or her previous rentals.

Your formal application should require prospective tenants to give written permission for you to conduct employment, bank, credit, background and reference checks. Depending on local custom, it may be appropriate to require the prospect to pay the reasonable costs of your research; $25 or $50 is fairly standard with online screening firms.

Dozens of companies perform tenant checks for landlords, and most can report back a basic profile in just moments. (Try searching "tenant background screening" at Yahoo! or Google.)

Typical profiles include credit and rental histories and employment information. Most firms can also conduct criminal background checks. You should pay to get a report on yourself or someone you know well to see how accurate or helpful the firm's research is.

Although these online background checks make the landlord's life immensely easier, don't rely on them 100 percent. Be skeptical. Big information databases are notoriously error ridden. Nothing beats doing your own due diligence. You won't be able to match a report from any of the big-three credit agencies, but there's no reason you can't call a prospect's current landlord or verify local employment on your own. You will learn a lot more talking person to person than you will from an e-mailed form.

Likewise, you need to come up with your own personal checklist of criteria for tenants and then apply them uniformly to all applicants. Example: It's perfectly OK to set as one of your criteria that an applicant can't have ever been in litigation with a landlord. But you have to stick to it. No exceptions.

All that said, if you decide not to rent to a prospect, you owe it to him or her to explain why in a timely manner. A simple telephone call ("You don't make enough money to afford this apartment") will usually suffice. But you should make notes on the application form, attach any supporting documents and keep it all on file. You never know when someone may complain about your decision.

If you do come across someone who makes a habit of taking landlords to court, you should take great care to explain in writing why you have rejected the application. (Language note: You didn't reject the *person,* only the *application.*) You don't have to be verbose, but you do need to be exact: "Your application was rejected due to information provided by XYZ Checking Service" or ". . . due to a reported history of damage to rental properties" or ". . . because of a reported history of adverse relations with neighbors." Be prepared for follow-up questions from the applicant. And take notes.

So what about the good applications?

If you have a choice among equally good applicants, all of whom have great jobs, steady rental histories, neat appearances, courteous demeanors, no debts, no bad histories and plenty of savings, then pick one any way you wish. You can take the earliest applicant. You can select the one whose information was verified first. You can even close your eyes and throw darts at the applications.

The important thing is to be consistent and not arbitrary or subjective. You will leave yourself open to a discrimination complaint if you make your decision strictly because you "feel" better about one applicant, or you think that other tenants might "get along" better with one over the other.

Besides, if these other applicants are so good, you don't want to risk alienating them and lose the opportunity of renting to them in the future.

ADVERTISING

Advertising your vacant house or apartment should be a snap. Read this fictional ad, however, and see if you can figure out why it's not:

"Small apartment. Ideal for young, single woman. No children. $800."

The landlord who placed this ad must have been watching his dollars. With only 10 words, it came in at just the right length for the weekly free newspaper's super-saver discount. Too bad that five of those words could end up costing the landlord—and possibly the paper—tens of thousands of dollars in damages, fines, court costs and legal fees.

You can't legally discriminate in your advertising on the basis of age, marital status or gender. That means you can't advertise that you are looking for a "young," "single" "woman," and you can't specify "no children."

As more apartments and houses are being rented through free weeklies, Internet ads, e-mails, online bulletin boards or off-line bulletin boards at the neighborhood coffee bar, property owners need to be careful with what they say in their advertising. You may have only the most benign of intentions, but that will not cut it with local housing authorities, rent boards or other government agencies charged with enforcing anti-discrimination, equal-opportunity laws. In February 2006, Craigslist was hit with a lawsuit from the Chicago Lawyers' Committee for Civil Rights Under Law, a fair-housing group, that accused the online listings giant of violating the Fair Housing Act by running discriminatory housing listings featuring comments such as "African Americans and Arabians tend to clash with me so that won't work out." Fortunately, major newspapers are geared to reject discriminatory wording, saving both the paper and the advertiser untold legal difficulties.

Your advertising will be most effective if you stick to describing the property, not the tenant. For example:

"Small apartment. Hot, trendy neighborhood. Safe. Walk to subway. $800."

With 10 words like that, you will attract plenty of young, single women. And you lost the people with kids at "small."

LEASES

Leases are your assets. Take great care with them.

Leases are the actual instruments with which your buildings, and you, make money. They don't just set the terms between landlord and tenant. They also create the value of the property itself, because an investment building's market value is a multiple of the income it generates. If you ever expect to sell your building, you will have to document its income with written leases or rental agreements.

Many small-property landlords get by with printed leases from the stationery store and then scribble in a few extra lines that suit them. That's OK, as long as you don't have any problems. But if it turns out that you have rented to the tenant from hell (think of the Michael Keaton character in the real-estate investor's horror flick, *Pacific Heights*), you will wish you had paid more attention to the rental terms. Better to do it right the first time.

Again, this is what your lawyer is for. A good real-estate attorney should have a standard, rock-solid lease that incorporates local law and customs and can be individualized for your use. If it saves you one hearing in housing court (as it's known in some places), the cost will be worth it. (See the appendix for a sample lease prepared by the Michigan legislature and printed in the excellent state publication *Tenants and Landlords: A Practical Guide,* available for downloading.)

There are plenty of items that you will want to make sure get addressed, such as pets, business activities, parking and common areas. Here are a few of the biggies.

- **Who's living in your building.** You want the name of every adult in the rental property to be on the lease, and you want them each to sign. This makes everyone living in the building responsible for all terms, including the full amount of the rent. You should also limit occupancy to only those adults named on the lease and their minor children. No new roommates or no new boyfriends or girlfriends without getting their names on the lease. No subletting. No "cousins" from Albuquerque.

- **How long the lease runs.** Leases typically run for a year or two, although there's nothing inherently wrong with even longer leases, provided they are enforceable and include annual rent kickers and whatever other adjustments may be necessary. In any case, you should spell out the length of the lease and stick to it. Some landlords prefer "rental agreements," which usually run from month to month and can be ended by either the landlord or tenant. If that's what you prefer, make sure the termination procedure is clearly spelled out.

- **The rent and when and how you want it.** You need to state the amount of the monthly rent and the day of the month it's due. You also need to specify how you want to be paid (check, money order, cash, etc.) along with the terms for late payments.

- **What's going on with the security deposit.** Spell out the exact amount of the security deposit (usually one month's rent; remember to increase the deposit when rents increase) and what it covers. Security deposits should cover damage and misuse matters; they shouldn't be used to pay the last month's rent. Make that clear in the lease. The lease should specify whether the deposit is held in an interest-bearing account (required in some states) and under what circumstances it will be refunded. Also remember to point out whatever other fees you might insist on: pets, cleaning, keys and so on.

- **Who's responsible for what.** The lease should clearly delineate what you are required to do and what the tenant is required to do. Generally, you should agree to regular maintenance and to make all repairs in a timely manner. The tenant should agree to keep the property clean and to pay for any damage that results from abuse. You also want to restrict the tenant's ability to make repairs or alterations without your approval.

- **The difference between home and property.** A tenant has the right to privacy in his or her home, but the lease should explicitly lay out the circumstances in which you can enter the rental unit. Likewise, the lease should state that use of the property for any illegal activity terminates the tenancy. Even broader, the tenant can be required to keep the place clean and to live in a quiet, neighborly manner that does not disturb other tenants or neighbors.

- **Terms of renewal.** Many tenants may want some assurance that they won't have to leave the apartment or their rent won't skyrocket at the end of their lease. Noncommittal oral assurances on your part are fine ("I'm sure we'll be able to work out something mutually agreeable when it's time to re-new"), but you will want to avoid any written commitments that could bind you beyond the specific terms of the lease. You don't want to end up with problem tenants who have clauses in their leases that may be interpreted as saying they have an automatic right to renew their tenancies.

MONEY

You owe it to yourself to maintain your rents at market levels. The value of your property is determined by its income. If you don't consistently raise rents in line with other comparable properties, your building will not appreciate as you would like. You shouldn't gouge your tenants, of course, but steady 3 per-cent to 5 percent annual increases have been reasonable in this economic environment. Rents for vacant and improved apartments can be raised considerably more.

You want to collect your rents on the first day of the month so that you can make your own monthly obligations in a con-sistent, businesslike manner. Don't have leases that run from mid-month to mid-month. If a tenant moves in at mid-month, prorate the first month's rent.

Tenants should pay rent with automatic transfers from their banks, checks, money orders, cash or debit cards. Small-property owners should be wary of accepting credit cards. Credit-card payments cost you because the card issuer charges landlords a transaction fee of 2 percent or 3 percent of the rent. If you do accept credit cards, you should charge the ten-ant a premium to cover the transaction fees. (Debit-card is-suers also charge landlords a fee, but it is much, much lower.)

Charge a substantial penalty for late rental payments, but also encourage early payments with modest discounts. No one paying $800 a month rent will be deterred by a $25 late fee. Spell out in the lease that the first late payment costs 10 percent and the second 15 percent. (Caution: Some states have caps on late fees.) Make three late payments in one year cause for eviction. Likewise, you should encourage direct deposit of rents, electronic funds transfers and even checks or cash delivered before the first of the month with discounts or refunds. For example: It could be well worth a 3 percent annual refund to have a "forgetful" tenant put you on an automatic payment through his or her bank. You'd have a guaranteed early rent payment and lose just $24 a month on that $800 apartment, while the tenant would be encouraged by anticipating a nice check from you just before Christmas.

Deposits are not your money; they belong to your tenants. Many states require that you keep them in a separate account, away from the account that you use to operate your business, and pay market-rate interest. When you sell your building, you will be expected to deliver the deposits to the new owner.

Deposits are refundable. A security deposit, which is paid at the time the lease is signed, is intended to cover extraordinary damage to the unit or furnishings and extraordinary cleaning. Some states allow for "nonrefundable" deposits for cleaning, pets and other matters, but these are more accurately described as "fees," not deposits.

A security deposit is not the last month's rent. Many tenants try to slip by with this offer: "Just take the security deposit for the rent." No way. The deposit must cover matters not covered by the rent. Otherwise, you could end up with a filthy, vacant apartment and no deposit to use to have it cleaned. (Security deposits are also good insurance for you. If a tenant should skip out in the middle of the night, you do have the deposit to cover the unpaid rent.)

MAINTENANCE

They broke it; you fix it.

There is no more fundamental duty of a landlord than to see that the building is properly maintained and that repairs are made promptly. It is no more acceptable to ask a tenant to live with a broken air conditioner or a leaky faucet than it is for a tenant to ask you to go without a rent check. They pay; you perform.

That said, you'd prefer to avoid performing as a 24-hour, seven-day-a-week repair service. Yes, emergencies happen— pipes burst in the middle of the night—and there's nothing you can do but get those things fixed immediately. But, fortunately, most maintenance can be handled in a more routine manner.

Set aside so many hours each week for repairs and maintenance and then have the tenants sign up for the handyman's or your time. Some repairs might require an outside contractor.

Fortunately, most repairs can wait a day or two—or more— so you can practice triage. Fix the more serious problems first, then the less serious. Apartment 2B's clogged toilet trumps 4C's loose cabinet-door hinge.

Another thing you can do to minimize your repair headaches is to routinely perform preventative maintenance and checkups. You should write in your lease that you will conduct semiannual maintenance inspections on air conditioners, heating units, refrigerators and the like to clean or replace filters, lubricate or do whatever else may be necessary. Simply brushing out a clothes dryer vent twice a year can prevent a fire, and replacing a cracked window in the dry summer can forestall water damage to the windowsill in winter. (While you're at it, don't forget to check up on the common areas, such as the storage room or the garage.)

Tenants will welcome a landlord who pays such close attention to their apartments. That's good for you, as happy tenants tend to remain paying tenants. But there's another benefit for you that the tenant may not realize. Those routine maintenance checkups can also help you keep up with what's going on in your units—whether new persons have moved in, whether the tenant is using the apartment for a business, whether the tenant is taking good care of the place. These are things that might be difficult for you to see if you weren't making routine maintenance inspections of the properties.

TENANT DISPUTES

Finally, it's time to put on your top hat and twirl your mustache.

No one likes to be the heavy in any relationship, but a landlord will occasionally need to play one. No matter how careful you are at selecting your tenants, you will pick bad ones from time to time. That nice young couple will break up, and one of them will stay in the apartment but not make enough money alone to pay the rent. The shy, quiet guy in 2C will fall in love with a woman who is into heavy metal bands and Saint Bernards. The little old lady in 1B turns out to have a crack-dealing nephew.

This is all very serious stuff. No matter how much you personally like your tenants, your relationships with them must remain strictly business. You must protect yourself and your investment. You must require these people to abide by the terms of their leases, or they must leave. There is no middle ground.

This point of view must be enforced from your first meeting with a prospective tenant. Your rules and procedures—rents are due on the first day of the month, no extra cars in the parking lot, no "roommates" not on the lease—protect your interests. You don't have to be a jerk about it, but you do need to be firm and consistent. If your standard lease says "no pets," that means no pets for everyone. And if someone turns up with a new puppy, you have to enforce your rules: Either the puppy goes or the tenant goes.

A landlord's ultimate weapon is, of course, eviction, the culmination of a costly and time-consuming legal process that invokes the power of the government to force someone to leave your building. Eviction procedures vary greatly from state to state, so we will go into only as much detail as necessary to sketch out the process. Suffice it to say, every day that you are involved evicting a tenant is a day that you are not making money. The out-of-pocket costs of an eviction are nominal, but the loss of income can be substantial if, say, one of your four units is tied up for three months while you try to get a deadbeat out.

So what we do want to do is look at some alternatives to eviction when dealing with troublesome tenants. Remember, you don't want an empty apartment. You want a tenant who is paying on time and living by your rules. Throughout your dealings, however, the shadow of an eviction proceeding must loom large. That's your nuclear option, and the recalcitrant tenant must believe that you are crazy enough to use it.

There are three broad reasons that landlords and tenants come to loggerheads: (1) The tenant has broken some term of the lease; (2) the tenant hasn't paid the rent; or (3) the term of the lease or rental agreement has expired and you wish to reclaim the property.

Failure to pay rent is certainly the most obvious and, from your point of view, the most immediate problem you can have. But it's the first reason, breaking lease terms, where you are far more likely to have difficulties. Tenants don't always read a lease closely. Interpretations of clauses and terms can vary. They may feel *you* are violating lease terms by not living up to your obligations as the landlord, giving them leeway to violate terms as well. A tenant may feel justified withholding rent payments if you have not followed through on promised repairs or improvements. A tenant may even feel he or she can pay for repairs that you haven't done and then deduct the cost from rent payments.

Many of these problems just get out of hand. Here are some things you can do to keep control.

- **Publish.** The simplest way to solve a tenant dispute is to avoid having one in the first place. Keep your tenants informed about what's going on around their homes—when painters are coming, when the roof is being repaired, when you'll be around for minor maintenance matters. Consider a building Web site or just a photocopied newsletter that keeps people filled in. Remind them of lease obligations as you point out what you are doing to make their homes better.

- **Talk.** Specific problems with specific tenants should be addressed one-on-one. Telephones are fine at first, but face-to-face meetings reinforce the seriousness of the issue. Remember to follow up. If you give a tenant through the weekend to correct a problem, be sure you speak again on Monday.

- **Write.** You've just escalated the matter to Def Con 2. If the problem is not solved after your talk, you must get the tenant's attention with a "notice to quit." The formal name of this legal document varies from state to state, but this notice is the first step in the eviction process. It informs the tenant that he or she has so many days (usually between three days and two weeks) to pay the back rent or to honor the terms of the lease or move out.

Here's where we want to diverge a bit. There are several paths you can take short of formal eviction.

- **Mediation.** Many communities offer free landlord-tenant mediation services and for-hire mediators are readily available as well. If the landlord and the tenant agree to abide by the mediation, most conflicts can be worked out after just an hour-long session. Warning: This is not arbitration, where a third party hears both sides and then imposes a settlement. Mediators work to bring both sides to an agreement. Mediation is not binding; if it fails to satisfy both parties legal options are still open.

- **Money.** There's nothing wrong with offering to grease the skids. If you want someone out of your building, and they aren't getting the message, consider offering some cash. An eviction can easily take four to eight weeks, and a determined deadbeat might be able to stretch that out for another couple of months. That could mean four months without rent coming in. So offer an appropriate amount of money if the tenant agrees to move out by a certain date. If you get control of your unit back after just a couple of weeks instead of a couple of months, the "incentive" that you paid would be worth it.

- **Muscle.** No, you can't hire Tony Soprano. But in many places you can hire the local sheriff's department to have a uniformed officer deliver legal papers, beginning with the notice to quit. Many sheriffs' offices post a fee schedule on their Web sites for these services. Many jurisdictions also allow off-duty officers to wear uniforms, so you can hire an individual to do your delivery.

What you can't do is retaliate. States have very specific laws outlining what landlords can't do when they are in disputes with tenants. Basically, you can't violate the "habitability" of the property—no changing of locks, no throwing people's possessions out on the curb, no turning off of utilities.

Don't even think about it.

CHAPTER 9

REAL ESTATE ON WALL STREET

REITs

*We buy businesses I can understand. . . . There are all kinds
of businesses I don't understand. I don't worry about that.
Why should I? Buy pieces of businesses you can understand
when they're offered to you for quite a bit less than they're
worth. That's all there is to it.*

— WARREN BUFFETT

Being a landlord isn't for everyone. It takes a certain
type of person to hound deadbeats for the back rent,
to put up drywall and install kitchen cabinets, or to spend Sat-
urdays fixing leaky faucets or interviewing new tenants. Being
a property investor can be a drag.

Fortunately, for would-be real-estate investors, there's an
easier—if more taxing—way of investing in real estate. Call
your stockbroker. There's real estate on Wall Street, too.

But be warned: Buying shares of real-estate companies on sale in the stock market is not real-estate investing. It's stock investing. And as we said earlier, there are fundamental differences between putting your money in stocks and investing in real estate.

Unlike a landlord, a stock investor has no power to materially affect the performance of his investment. Successful real-estate investing requires your active participation in the management of your properties. Stock investing requires careful research and due diligence. But once you've paid for the stock, all you can do is keep an eye on it. You can buy more when you think you should; you can sell it when you made—or lost—enough.

In this chapter, we will be looking at some of these less-hands-on ways of investing in real estate, principally investments in companies that specialize in real-estate development and related activities: REITs (real-estate investment trusts), home builders and building-products companies. These are the public companies that most profited from the real-estate boom, and, surprisingly, remain relatively well positioned to ride out a far less frenetic future.

We will look at some of the major players in the fields, show how these types of businesses operate and demonstrate how to evaluate them from an investor's point of view. We'll also look briefly at some of the more sophisticated real-estate-related investments in mortgage-backed securities and other financial instruments.

So let's start where most real-estate activity on Wall Street takes place.

WHAT'S A REIT ANYWAY?

And what does it do? And can it keep doing it?

REITs are corporations that develop, acquire and operate properties. They are prodigious cash machines, developing, owning and operating various types of properties while churn-

INVESTORS, BEWARE

Some words of caution: You may already own a lot of real estate in your stock portfolio.

Stock investors seeking to diversify their holdings with real estate need to be aware of just how dependent they already are on it. In the uncertain real-estate world we are now facing, your exposure to a potentially declining asset base of properties will be coming from directions you are not necessarily watching.

You are already heavily invested in real estate if you own stocks or corporate bonds, if you hold any mutual funds in your 401(k) or IRA, if your retirement nest egg is in a traditional pension fund or if you have life insurance. Even your 10-year-old's savings account is a real-estate investment of sorts, since the bank lends that money out in the form of residential and commercial mortgages. Real estate underpins the economy, and when property values decline they can do great damage. One word: Japan.

Holding different types of stocks in your portfolio at the same time (diversification) is a time-honored investing practice that helps to minimize your risk by reducing your exposure to any one type of stock investment. Diversified investors weathered the technology meltdown far better than investors heavily betting on tech stocks. It is a big unknown, however, what impact a prolonged real-estate slump could have on stock prices.

A 1999 study in the *Journal of Corporate Real Estate* estimated that 40 percent of publicly owned corporations' assets were land and buildings. Mutual funds, too, are deep in the real-estate sector. One 2005 study found that the average so-called large-cap mutual fund had 4 percent of its holdings tied to real estate. Typical "value" funds were in much deeper, as much as 17 percent for some fund groups.

CalPERS, the mammoth California Public Employees' Retirement System, has about $11 billion in real-estate investments. About 8 percent of the Pennsylvania public-employees' pension fund is in direct real-estate holdings.

Fortunately, the real-estate bubble didn't lead many companies to refashion themselves as property developers—the way some old industrial companies redefined themselves in the 1990s as tech firms in order to ride the technology bubble.

Still, just as homeowners basked in the psychological wealth effect created by rising real-estate prices, corporations, too, enjoyed a run-up in the paper values of their real-estate assets. Wal-Mart's balance sheets, for instance, registered a 31 percent increase in the value of the corporation's land, buildings and fixtures from 2003 to 2005, when the retailing giant was rapidly closing its signature discount stores and opening even bigger "supercenters." The total number of Wal-Mart stores increased only 9 percent in that period; net sales went up 24 percent.

ing out high dividends to their investors. And REIT stocks, which are traded just like any other stocks, performed quite well over the first half of the decade.

They have done so well, in fact, that the top REIT-investing trend lately has been the cash-out—publicly traded firms going private. Among the big deals: The Blackstone Group, a top-tier private equity firm, agreed to buy office-building developer CarrAmerica Realty Corporation for about $5.6 billion, an 18 percent premium over the price of its public shares. Morgan Stanley paid 20 percent over the stock price to acquire luxury apartment landlord AMLI Residential Properties Trust.

In all, more than $15 billion in such deals were made during 2005 and early 2006. And ironically, the dual drives to sell out and to acquire were both fueled by the fickle nature of the real-estate bubble. The sellers saw real-estate topping out, while the buyers saw a lag between the stock prices of the REITs and the values of their properties. In other words, the properties owned by the REITs were worth more than the stock price reflected. The private real-estate firms saw that buying a REIT outright was a quick and economical way to pick up properties below market.

"You have all of these factors combining to push money into real estate," Dale Anne Reiss, who runs the real-estate practice for Ernst & Young, told my *Wall Street Journal* colleague

TYPES OF REITS

Equity REITs. Equity REITs own and operate properties and engage in a wide range of real-estate activities, including leasing, development and management.

Mortgage REITs. Mortgage REITs lend money directly to real-estate owners and operators or extend credit indirectly through the acquisition of loans or mortgage-backed securities.

Hybrid REITs. A hybrid REIT both owns properties and makes loans to real-estate owners and operators.

Source: National Association of Real Estate Investment Trusts

∽

Christine Haughney. "An event like this presents an opportunity for investors and executives to cash out."

REIT BASICS

We will be concentrating here on "equity REITs," the largest, most widely known real-estate companies.

REITs don't buy single-family homes, but they do own nearly all other types of income-producing properties. They usually, though not always, specialize in specific types of buildings— multifamily, office, health care, industrial and the like, and then often in subspecialties such as apartments or mobile-home parks, self-storage facilities or manufacturing centers. Some companies called "diversified REITs" will own various types of properties. There are about 200 publicly traded REITs with a combined market value of $300 billion.

REITs generally are valued based on a certain measure of cash flow called "adjusted funds from operations" (AFFO), which computes the money the REIT makes and then modi-

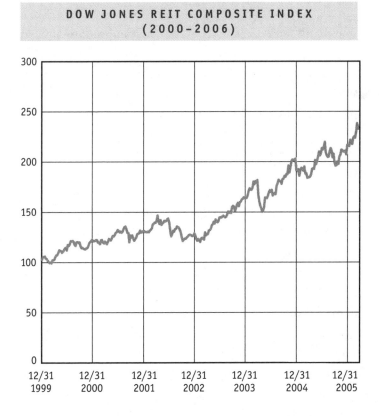

DOW JONES REIT COMPOSITE INDEX (2000–2006)

fies it with what it pays for upkeep of its properties. That, rather than reported earnings, is the main benchmark because investors recognize that most properties don't lose value over time, and the depreciation charged against reported profits is a phantom expense.

As with any stock, an investor buys a REIT with the expectation that it will increase in value over time—cash flow and earnings will go up, and with that, so will the price of the stock. One way of expressing that is when you buy a stock—any stock— you are buying a claim on the company's future earnings. That is as true for Google, which presumably will justify its stratospheric stock price with ever increasing profits, as it is for a slow-growth, old-line industrial giant paying a generous dividend.

For various reasons, however, REIT investors are making a substantial claim on current as well as future earnings. Until the big real-estate price run-up, few people bought REIT stocks with the expectation of rapid price appreciation. What they bought was the expectation of a hefty quarterly check.

That's because REITs are distinguished by an unusual tax status that exempts the corporation from income taxes while requiring it to pass along the great bulk of its income directly to shareholders. A typical blue-chip stock may have a dividend yield of 1 percent or 2 percent, but a REIT may pay out 4 percent, 5 percent or often much more. So, REITs traditionally were viewed mainly as income-producing investments.

That changed because of some significant changes to tax laws made earlier in this decade. While REIT dividends generally run higher than other corporate payouts, REIT dividends aren't eligible for the 15 percent dividend tax rate put in place in 2003. That means REIT investors generally pay taxes on most of their dividends at higher, ordinary income rates. Example: A well-to-do investor receiving a $1 dividend from a REIT should expect to pay about 35 cents in income taxes, while an investor in a typical corporation will pay just 15 cents to the IRS.

After the tech-stock crash in 2000, REITs turned out to be one of the safest ports in the storm. Bolstered by their generous dividends—promising investors real money in their pockets to replace the worthless tech stocks—REIT shares performed admirably during the 2000–2002 bear market. The Dow Jones Composite REIT Index almost tripled after January 2000. Indeed, the REIT Index has not been lower since. It rose steadily throughout the bear market (up almost 30 percent as the NASDAQ Composite Index was falling nearly 80 percent), and then it rocketed upward after the tax law changed, interest rates began falling and the real-estate market took off. REITs continued to go up through most of 2006.

SPREADING YOUR BETS

Still, it's all relative. Just as not all buildings perform the same functions, not all REITs are made the same way. Real estate

FIVE LARGEST REITS	
Big Property Owners	**Market Cap ($ Mil)**
Simon Property Group, Inc.	16,384.0
Equity Office Properties Trust	13,300.4
Vornado Realty Trust	12,157.6
General Growth Properties, Inc.	10,673.3
Equity Residential	10,604.8

Source: National Association of Real Estate Investment Trusts

and REITs are segmented into many different sorts of properties, and stock prices across segments don't always move together. As a group, for instance, the stocks of REITs specializing in residential properties outperformed office REITs in the first five years of the decade. But both sectors trailed well behind REITs specializing in retail properties.

Two important lessons for investors: It rarely hurts to spread your bets; diversified REITs that invest in different types of properties as a rule outperformed more specialized companies. And before you buy a REIT stock, check what Treasury bonds are paying. Among the top performers in the residential, office, retail and diversified-REIT investing sectors, only six stocks had dividend yields greater than 8 percent at 2005's market-topping prices; many were in the 3 percent to 5 percent range. (All REIT dividends averaged just 4.5 percent, while Treasurys were paying about 4.2 percent.)

So diversification is a good thing. And there are two ways to get it: You can invest in one company with a broad portfolio of properties (a diversified REIT), or you can invest in a mutual fund that specializes in REITs and real-estate-related investments.

According to the Morningstar research firm, the top performer among *all* mutual funds for the first five years of the century was the Alpine U.S. Real Estate Equity Fund. From the stock-market peak in early 2000 to mid-2005, the fund's growth averaged an astounding 34 percent a year. Put another way, if

SPREADING YOUR BETS	
Largest Real-Estate Mutual Funds	**Total Assets ($ Mil)**
Vanguard REIT Index	6,756
Fidelity Real Estate Investment	5,821
Third Avenue Real Estate Value	2,962
Cohen & Steers Realty Shares	2,042
DFA Real Estate Securities	1,769

Source: Morningstar

you had sold half of your $20,000 worth of Pets.com stock on the day the NASDAQ market peaked and bought Alpine shares, your real-estate investment would be worth more than $40,000 today, while your remaining Pets.com stock certificates could be used to line your cat's litter box.

HOME BUILDERS AND BUILDING PRODUCTS

Samuel Lieber, the manager of the Alpine real-estate fund, engineered his startling run-up by concentrating not on REITs, but on home builders. And he was still bullish on them in mid-2006.

"We don't see a bubble," he told my *Barron's* magazine colleague Christopher C. Williams. "Historically, home prices just don't go down nationwide unless we are in a significant recession. The underlying fundamentals of real estate are still very positive." His number one home-building stock pick? Lennar Corporation, which was selling in the low $60s in mid-2006, and which Mr. Lieber thinks has the potential to hit $80 a share by 2008. (By late 2006, the stock was in the mid-$40s.)

While home builders have proven to be a good long-term investment—the Dow Jones U.S. Home Construction Index has risen an average of 29 percent every year since 1994—the individual home builders have been a notoriously fickle lot. Their stock performance is intimately associated with the overall economy, local economies in the areas where they concentrate their efforts and interest rates.

So, once again, diversification works in the investor's favor.

BIG BUILDERS	
Largest Home Builders	**Market Cap ($ Mil)**
Pulte Homes Inc.	9,674
D.R. Horton Inc.	9,672
Lennar Corp.	8,967
Centex Corp.	8,206
Toll Brothers	5,945
KB Home	5,462

Concentrate on companies that operate in more than one geographic region and aren't exposed to the ups and downs of one region's economy. Toll Brothers, for example, has a large presence in the Washington, D.C., area, while KB Home, which is strong in California, has been expanding in the Southeast and the Midwest.

Even with a deflating real-estate market, there is still going to be demand for new homes. The regions that saw the great price run-ups early in the decade—California, Florida and the Northeast—are almost certain to see stagnation and even price declines, but much of the rest of the country still has plenty of investment potential. In its *The State of the Nation's Housing: 2005* report, Harvard University's Joint Center for Housing Studies saw no impending decline in the start of new-home construction. Harvard's economists found that the inventory of new homes for sale today, measured against the pace of home sales, is near its lowest level ever.

"Given this small backlog, new-home sales would have to retreat by more than a third—and stay there for a year or more—to create anywhere near a buyer's market," the study said.

As you might expect, construction companies and the companies that supply them with building materials mutually benefit each other. Home-building companies use lots of wood, concrete, pipe, electrical wires, glass, kitchen cabinets, plumbing fixtures and thousands of other components to build a modern suburban home or building. And the stocks of the

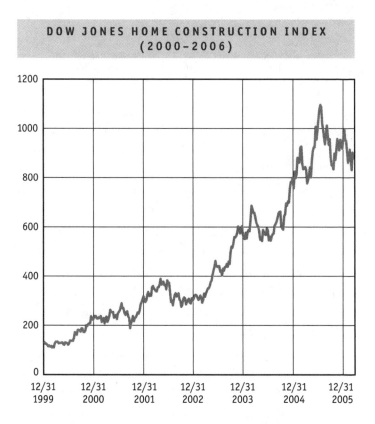

DOW JONES HOME CONSTRUCTION INDEX (2000–2006)

building-products makers had very healthy price increases through the real-estate boom.

In 2003, the last year for which estimates exist, owners of homes and rental buildings spent $233 billion on improving their properties, and the U.S. building boom contributed to worldwide commodity price increases for basic building prod-

SUPPLY CHAIN

Largest Building-Products Companies	Market Cap ($ Mil)
Cemex S.A.	18,997
Lafarge	14,441
CRH plc	13,554
Masco Corp.	12,244
Rinker Group	10,377

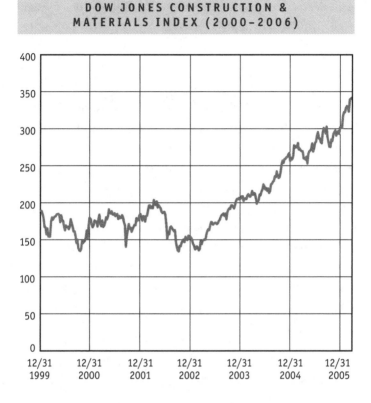

DOW JONES CONSTRUCTION & MATERIALS INDEX (2000–2006)

ucts. Plywood and cement logged 40 percent year-to-year price increases mid-decade.

PAPER PROFITS

Two great government initiatives have made homes Americans' preferred asset. The first sparked a social revolution; the second a financial one.

Immediately after World War II the federal government guaranteed down-payment-free 30-year mortgages to veterans, turning a generation raised as urban renters into suburban homeowners. Following the ex-GIs, their wives and their boom of babies came mass-produced communities of single-family homes, the Interstate Highway System, shopping centers and, eventually, office and industrial developments. In 1940, on the eve of America's entry into the war, only about 43 percent of

Americans lived in owner-occupied dwellings. Thirty years later, in 1970, the number was 63 percent.

That's when Ginnie Mae, the Government National Mortgage Association, sparked a financial revolution with the introduction of "mortgage-backed securities." MBSs made mortgages "liquid," easily traded financial instruments that could be readily bought and sold, like stocks and bonds, and assured a steady supply of money for home buyers, even when individual lenders might have been disinclined to make mortgage loans.

The main disadvantage that real-estate investors face is the "illiquid" nature of their investments. With an apartment house, you can't go online, enter a few keystrokes, sell it and bank the proceeds by the end of the day, all for a modest broker fee. Until the dawn of the MBS era, banks and other lenders faced a similar problem. If they made a mortgage and loaned a homeowner money, they were pretty much stuck with the loan until it was paid off, or not. If interest rates rose, which they did mightily from the late 1960s through the early 1980s, lower interest loans became drags on lenders. They were borrowing new money at rates higher than they were receiving for older mortgage loans.

Enter mortgage-backed securities. MBSs greatly reduced the risk that lenders faced making long-term loans amid volatile interest rates. Ginnie Mae, a government agency, and two government-sponsored companies, the Federal National Mortgage Association (Fannie Mae) and the Federal Home Loan Mortgage Corporation (Freddie Mac), buy mortgage loans from banks, mortgage companies and other originators, assemble the loans into "pools" and then issue securities that represent claims on the principal and interest payments of the loans, a process known as securitization. Some private institutions, such as brokerage firms, banks, and home builders, also securitize mortgages, known as "private-label" mortgage securities.

These types of bonds are not cheap. Most are sold in denominations of $25,000. Individual investors can purchase mortgage-backed securities at most major brokers and many

MY BANKER, MYSELF

 There is another way to play the mortgage market: become a lender yourself.

Private or "hard-money" lenders are small companies or individuals—doctors, lawyers, entrepreneurs, any high net-worth individuals—operating outside the traditional lending establishment.

Private lenders typically rely far more on the income-producing capacity of the property than on the credit worthiness of the borrower. Typical terms on a first mortgage for an income property: a one-year loan of no more than 65 percent of the price, an interest rate of 15 percent, and four loan-origination points. Terms on second mortgages usually go right up to the edge of state usury laws.

If you choose to go this route, you'll want to make sure you have an ironclad, enforceable mortgage contract. Under no circumstances should you lend more than 70 percent of the value of an income producing property. And the total debt-to-service ratio—the property's annual net operating income divided by annual debt service—should never fall below 1.0.

Lend on properties that will be easy to dispose of in case of loan default. Multitenant properties are generally preferable to single-tenant buildings.

---

discount brokers. Fidelity Investments has developed one of the most extensive bond trading operations for individuals (http://personal.fidelity.com/products/fixedincome).

For much less money, individuals can buy shares in mutual funds that hold the bonds. There are scores of funds that invest in MBSs. Morningstar, the mutual-fund ranking service, lists them under "intermediate government funds" (go to the fund screener at http://www.morningstar.com).

CHAPTER 10

Are You Rich Yet?

The 20 Things Every Real-Estate Investor Needs to Know

"My land. We're here and we're gonna stay here. Gimme ten years and I'll have that brand on the gates of the greatest ranch in Texas. The big house'll be down by the river, the corrals and the barns behind it. . . . But it takes work, it takes sweat, and it takes time, lots of time. It takes years."

—John Wayne
Red River (screenplay by Borden Chase,
Charles Schnee and Howard Hawks)

In this final chapter, we will recap many of the points raised throughout this book and try to encapsulate them into a coherent, unified theory of real-estate investing. No one's promising the property owner's equivalent of $E = mc^2$, but this should show you how to go about building a significant portfolio of profitable properties.

We begin where we started, where we unveiled the real "secret" of real-estate investing: There are no secrets.

From there we will raise a simple but necessary note of caution about one especially dangerous form of real-estate investing that lured many novices in the bubble era. Then, the ultimate review, what many of you skipped ahead to read—20 things every real estate investor needs to know, including, at the end, a final flourish: the one and only 100 percent guaranteed way that you and your family can achieve prosperity and financial freedom.

MORE SECRETS OF REAL-ESTATE INVESTORS

As we said when we started, anyone can learn how to make money in real estate because it's fairly easy to figure out. Here, again, are the four big "secrets" of property investing, restated and expanded upon:

- **You must always buy property at a discount.** Buy it for less than you could sell it for today. That's what Warren Buffett does with companies, and what you should do with buildings. Ideally, you should buy most properties for 30 percent or more below their current market value. You won't always be able to do that, of course, but the best way to make sure you'll make money at the end of a deal is to pay as little as possible in the beginning.

- **Use as much of other people's money as you can.** Borrow money to buy into an investment property, and have tenants cover all your operating costs and pay back your loans. Real estate is uniquely suited for leveraging investment funds because of its relative price stability, especially compared to stocks. Whether you borrow the money from a bank or bring in partners with deep pockets, you will maximize your financial return if you maximize your leverage. Your goal is to acquire a property's income, appreciation and tax benefits while risking as little of your own money as possible.

- **Make sure your property pays for itself.** Under no circumstances should a novice investor go into a deal with a negative cash flow. It is better to put too much money down and reduce your overall return than to try to own a property that requires extra money from you to keep operating. If you can't structure a deal in such a way that your building covers all its expenses with its own income, then don't buy it.

- **Take maximum advantage of the tax laws.** You are under no legal or moral obligation to pay one dollar of taxes more than the law requires. The government has chosen to favor real-estate investors with a variety of tax preferences, all of which contribute to the landlord's income and wealth. Because of these tax preferences, real-estate investors can expect to do far better over the long term than other investors.

One could easily argue that a fifth "secret" is to keep investing, keep building, keep growing. It's a lesson taught over and over. If you are serious about becoming a real-estate investor, quit living like a real-estate consumer. Scale back your living costs and use your money to make more money.

Invest and reinvest and reinvest again. Start with one property. Then buy another . . . then two more . . . then four more . . .

No one's suggesting that you can join the billionaires' club with a few rental properties, but even a modestly successful real-estate investor should be able to amass a million-dollar-plus fortune producing income in excess of comparable stock or bond investments.

A conservatively managed, well diversified $1 million stock and bond retirement portfolio should be expected to produce a pretax income of $50,000 to $70,000 a year. In most parts of the country, a $1 million investment in rental houses and apartment buildings would do better; $90,000 to $100,000 would not be an unreasonable expectation.

But the real money comes with volume, leverage and tax breaks. Don't forget: With just 20 percent of the price of a building, you buy 100 percent of its income, and the government mitigates your risks by cutting your income taxes.

Do the math. Remember those $110,000 two-family homes we looked at in Memphis? Remember that the two-unit buildings could be bought for just about the same cost as a single-family home in the same neighborhood?

We figured that the low-end rent for each unit would be about $500 a month and that with a 20 percent down payment ($22,000) the income—after all expenses, including mortgage payments—would be a modest $250 a month. That's not enough to retire on, but it is an annual return of 13.6 percent on your down payment.

You see where we're going? Multiply that kind of leverage and those numbers over 45 similar buildings, and you'll own 20 percent of properties worth a total of $5 million and 100 percent of real money-in-your-pocket income of $135,000 a year.

It gets better. Without a doubt, the greatest advantages that real-estate investing enjoys over traditional stocks-and-bonds investing are the tax preferences. Even in an era of 15 percent capital-gains tax rates, the dollar-for-dollar write-offs afforded to property owners can't be beat.

A person making a $135,000 salary would probably end up paying $20,000 to $25,000 a year in federal income taxes, plus $7,000 more in Social Security and Medicare taxes. A stock investor earning $135,000 a year in dividends would pay $20,000 a year in taxes.

The landlord's tax bill? About $1,800.

In this case, each of those 45 two-family houses will be depreciating about $2,600 a year, creating an annual paper loss of $117,000 and reducing the landlord's taxable income to just $18,000. The actual tax rate? Just 1 percent. In other words, the landlord would be living virtually income-tax free on an annual income of $135,000.

A stocks-and-bonds investor would need a portfolio worth

about $3.5 million to pocket that kind of after-tax money. And the always-doomed office worker would need a salary of about $170,000.

There is no more compelling argument for real-estate investing.

LEAVE YOUR IRA ALONE

A note of great caution.

As you get older, you may be fortunate enough to amass a sizable fortune in your IRA or 401(k). These funds may end up seeing you through your last 20 to 40 years of life. Don't dip into them incautiously.

As real estate bubbled through the first half of the decade, a disturbing trend took hold. It was a sure sign of the kind of buying mania that grips any market on the verge of correction. Many novice real-estate barons were encouraged to invest directly in properties through their traditional or Roth IRAs. A whole subset of retirement-fund custodian firms sprang up to facilitate the buying of properties through expensive "self-directed" IRAs and other tax-deferred plans. Some even advertised "checkbook" access to IRA funds.

We pointed out earlier that IRA funds can be a good source of money to buy a first home that is also an income property, but that is a different situation altogether. That's taking money out of your IRA (no penalty for a first-home buyer), paying the taxes due and holding the property in the traditional fashion.

But actually using the IRA money to directly invest in and own properties is, for most investors, a very bad idea. There are scenarios in which IRA funds can be invested successfully in properties, but few novice investors are likely to have sufficient funds in their IRAs to participate in such enterprises, and certainly not without dangerously concentrating their retirement funds' investment mix.

There are few advantages, and multiple disadvantages.

- **The IRS rules for retirement-fund investments in real estate are complex, and the penalties for doing it wrong are severe.** It may seem that the IRS is trying to discourage real-estate investment, but that's not the case. IRAs can legally invest in anything from raw land to condos. But the rules outlining "prohibited" transactions bar selling property to or buying it from your IRA, lending or borrowing IRA money, using any part of the IRA as security for a loan or receiving or providing any kinds of goods or services to the IRA. Failure to comply could result in some or all of the real-estate investment being declared a "contribution" and subject to immediate tax and, if you are under 59, an additional 10 percent penalty.

- **You will need to buy the property entirely with IRA funds, rely on untraditional and hard-to-get partial financing or enter into joint ownership arrangements.** The IRA cannot itself borrow money or take out a mortgage. That leaves you with little leverage and few financing options. You will have to use all IRA funds to buy a property or turn to an untraditional lender who will lend on a "nonrecourse" or essentially unsecured basis. An alternative would be to make the IRA a partner in the property with a nonfamily member (sons or daughters, no; brother or brother-in-law, yes) who puts up the balance of the purchase price.

- **Your ongoing expenses—all goods and services—will have to be paid only with IRA funds.** This must be a strict "hands-off" arrangement. You cannot use any personal money to fix a leaky roof, paint an empty apartment or hire a manager without running afoul of the "excess-contribution" rules. Nor can you do work on the property yourself as that, too, can be considered an excess contribution. Your IRA will have to pay outsiders—no family—for all leasing, management and maintenance matters.

- **You will enjoy no depreciation-related tax benefits while owning the property.** And capital gains, usually taxed at a 15 percent rate, and recovered depreciation, taxed at a 25 percent rate, will be paid at full income-tax rates, up to 35 percent, because that's how all traditional IRA money is taxed when you take a distribution. Adding insult to injury, if you should have to sell the IRA investment property at less than your cost basis, you will not be allowed to write off any of the loss.

- **Don't try this at home.** Neither you nor anyone in your family will have an opportunity to personally enjoy any of the benefits of owning the property. As long as the property is held by the IRA, no one in your immediate family—from your parents to your grandchildren—can live in the property or otherwise make use of it. If you buy a retirement home, for example, and rent it to someone else for 20 years, you can put the rental income in your IRA. But when you retire, you will have to take the house as a distribution before you can move in. That would leave you with a substantial tax bill, perhaps greater even than your original purchase price.

- **Finally, the illiquid nature of a real-estate investment could prove devastating to you in a prolonged, Japan-style real-estate slump.** For many people, their home has replaced the traditional company pension plan as the third "leg" in their retirement-planning stool—real estate, Social Security, savings (IRAs, etc.). To have two of those legs tied up in the same type of asset is to invite old-age poverty.

Those considerable negatives aside, there are some rare instances when an IRA might be an interesting property-investment mechanism. Consider the Roth IRA, for instance. A marvelous tax-avoidance vehicle, a Roth IRA lets you invest after-tax money that then grows tax free. Unlike a traditional IRA in which you invest tax-free money and pay income taxes upon taking money out, you never pay taxes on a Roth distribution. So, if you have enough money in a Roth to maintain a well-diversified investment mix and you comply with all the rules, an investment property held over a long period of time could provide some considerable heft to your net worth. Of course, that's a lot of ifs.

Another direct property investment that might be fruitful with an IRA is to provide the financial muscle in a partnership engaging in very quick property flips, if they take less than one year. If the IRA covers all the purchase, rehab and selling costs, it could cut down considerably on the time it takes to manage the flip—no waiting for bank approvals—and speed payback. Once again, you'd be required to follow the hands-off rules assiduously, but the payoff would come in an income-tax-free closing. (The profit from the sale of a property you have held for less than a year is taxed at regular income rates. Hold a property longer than a year, and the profit is taxed at the much lower capital-gains rate.)

All that aside, here's the best rule for novice investors considering direct property investing with an IRA: Don't.

WHAT EVERY REAL-ESTATE INVESTOR NEEDS TO KNOW

Since you have come this far, you deserve a simple wrap-up. Point by point, here are the 20 essential rules that any novice real-estate investor needs to know to be successful.

1. **Investing requires capital.** This is the antithesis of the "something-for-nothing" hucksters' message, which is generally built around the notion that you can get into real-estate investing with no money. You can't. It's called "capitalism" for a reason.

2. **Other people's money.** You needn't plan on carrying the whole load yourself. There are any number of sources of funds to purchase real estate. Lenders are open to real-estate deals that can show in advance that the property is or quickly can be made profitable.

3. **Investing is not the same as owning a home.** Most people think they are investing in real estate because they own a home. If that's the case then most people are not good real-estate investors. It is not at all uncommon for a home-owner to actually lose money on a property that has tripled or more in value. A good landlord, however, can turn any old money pit into a personal ATM.

4. **Providing one of the necessities of life is a good business.** Yes, everyone does have to live somewhere, work some-where or shop somewhere, and the real-estate investor profits handsomely by providing the space in which most of modern life takes place.

5. **It's who you know, what you know and how you know it.** Building a real-estate investment business is not a solo af-fair. You must cultivate a network of contacts to help you with the acquisition and operation of your properties. You must thoroughly investigate both the finances and physi-cal condition of any property you want to buy. And you must structure your purchase so that the building will op-erate profitably.

6. **Leverage is good; negatives are bad.** Even a highly lever-aged investor with a building that is paying for itself can expect to make significant profits in real estate. Negative cash flows, however, will sap your profits and tax your man-agement skills.

7. **The government favors real-estate investments.** For most people, taxes are their number one expense. But real-estate investors enjoy far more generous income-tax breaks than most other investors or salaried workers. And most of these loopholes are so deeply embedded into the system that they will likely survive future tax-law reforms, even flat-tax plans.

8. **Losses can be good.** By allowing landlords to write off fake "paper" depreciation losses against other income, the

government has created a mighty incentive for ordinary individuals to become real-estate investors. The bar for qualifying for these write-offs can be high, but the rewards in markedly reduced taxes are likely to be higher. For an investor with a primary job outside real estate, it would not be unusual to make more money from real-estate-related annual tax savings than from rents.

9. **Taxes deferred can become taxes never paid.** Real-estate investors can defer taxes on the sale of a property by participating in a special "1031 exchange." You can "trade up" to another property and defer your capital-gains tax. You can repeat the process indefinitely, and under certain circumstances, you might be able to avoid paying most or all of the deferred taxes forever.

10. **Residential properties are best for novice investors.** Easy lending practices make houses and small apartment buildings especially attractive for novice investors. Even a tiny "in-law" apartment attached to your home can be a good investment because it can greatly reduce the cost of home owning.

11. **Buy in areas you know.** Novice investors should avoid buying properties far away from where they live. There is no way you can effectively manage a building from hundreds of miles away. And when you do buy, buy near your home or office. As you expand your property holdings, keep your buildings close to each other.

12. **There's a buyers' market in small rental buildings.** Renters became homeowners by the millions during the real-estate boom. As a result, demand pushed home prices through the roof. But prices for two-, three- and four-family buildings did not rise so high, or so quickly. That means there are opportunities in those types of properties for investors.

13. **Commercial properties are not for newbies.** Acquisition costs, operating expenses and the need for experienced

management put most commercial buildings, including large multifamily residential properties, well beyond the means of novice investors.

14. **Pick a niche.** If you are determined to make a business in commercial properties, settle on an area of expertise, whether in larger residential buildings, offices, retail, industrial or whatever. Each operates differently and requires different management techniques. If you are interested in investing in land, then you should be prepared either to develop it yourself or to "bank" it for a time until other developers need to buy it.

15. **Get your hands dirty.** Successful real-estate investing is a hands-on business that requires your active participation. You should not expect to simply put your money down and collect the rewards. You need to know how your properties operate.

16. **Leases are assets.** Contracts that you sign with tenants create the value of your property. Take care to write strong leases that spell out exactly what you expect of your tenants and what they should expect from you. And hold your tenants to the lease terms. No exceptions.

17. **Know your rights, and your tenants' rights.** Landlord-tenant laws vary from state to state, and you are obligated to know what you can and cannot do where you operate your properties. You can't discriminate. But if you are careful selecting your tenants, you will greatly minimize future problems.

18. **There are opportunities in the markets.** There are three broad areas of the stock and bond markets in which real-estate investors can participate: real-estate investment trusts (REITs), builders and building-supply firms, and bonds issued by lenders such as Fannie Mae or Ginnie Mae. Given the huge run-up in share prices during the last five years, past levels of price appreciation may be difficult

to sustain. Investors should concentrate on income-producing stocks.

19. **Leave your IRA alone.** Novice investors should avoid using IRA funds for direct property investments. Although the government allows IRA real-estate investing, the rules are strict and difficult to follow. Furthermore, holding properties in an IRA negates most of the tax advantages of real-estate investing and, in effect, even raises the levies on capital gains because they will taxed as regular income.

20. **Make your own way to financial freedom.** There have been no "no-money-down" fantasies in this book. Rather, we have stressed the conservative virtues of saving and prudent real-estate investing. Anyone with a good job, energy and discipline should be able to make use of enough of this book to build for him or herself a very nice life, both materially rich and spiritually satisfying.

You can have a good home, there will be plenty of money for your kids' educations, you can contribute generously to the community, your retirement can be financially comfortable and you can expect to pass along an estate worth far more than you might otherwise have dreamed possible.

In short, you can have financial independence.

What you cannot have, however, is all of that and the biggest, newest, fanciest house in town, the biggest car, the longest yacht, the priciest jewelry, the finest couture gowns, the best wines or the grandest vacations.

Don't confuse spending a lot of money with having a lot of money. No one ever got rich or stayed rich by spending.

The real-estate hucksters and schemers don't want you to know that. They dominate the bestseller lists and late-night TV hours peddling a vulgar, upside-down vision of wealth. Like con artists, they seduce their dreaming, gullible marks in the get-rich-quick crowd with images of the unsupportable lifestyles of not simply the idle rich, but the indolent, petted, parasitic rich, the kind of rich people who give wealth a bad name.

This fetishism of extravagance is reinforced day in and day out on television, in movies, in books and magazines, and even in some newspapers.

It's a fantasy that is rarely challenged—or balanced, even—with views of the tens of thousands of people who have amassed considerable riches by resisting the domination of the consumerist spending culture.

The vast majority of rich people are distinguished by one overwhelming, dominant trait: They're frugal. They drive old cars, live in modest houses and wear average clothes. They are rich, not because they are lucky or they have found some secret formula to wealth, but because they work hard, keep a long-term perspective and spend little.

And that's not something investing gurus want to tell you. No huckster ever got you to give him your money by telling you not to. And since most hucksters are not in a customer-service business—they are in a customer-exploiting business—they are not going to tell you the real secret of investing success.

They are not going to share with you the one and only guaranteed path to financial freedom: *Save your money.*

Then use the rules and techniques in this book—and learn more from other books, Web sites and mentors—to build a well-rounded, diversified investment portfolio for you and your family.

That should include stocks and bonds, to be sure. But build your family fortune, the one you want to last 200 years, on real bedrock. Property. Bricks and mortar. Steel and glass. Land. Real estate.

GET IT IN WRITING

This is a sample residential lease prepared by the Michigan legislature and printed in the excellent state publication *Tenants and Landlords: A Practical Guide*. Download at http://www.legislature.mi.gov; click on "Publications" in the left column.

RESIDENTIAL LEASE AGREEMENT

NOTICE:

**Michigan law establishes rights and obligations
for Parties to rental agreements.
This agreement is required to comply
with the Truth in Renting Act.
If you have a question about the interpretation
or legality of a provision of this agreement,
you may want to seek assistance from a lawyer
or other qualified person.**

We Agree That

_____

(Landlord's Name[s])

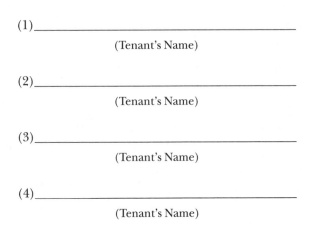

Leases To

(1) _____

(Tenant's Name)

(2) _____

(Tenant's Name)

(3) _____

(Tenant's Name)

(4) _____

(Tenant's Name)

**The Following Premises To Be Used For
Private Residential Purposes Only**

_____

(Street Address, City, State, and Zip Code)

For A Term

Beginning _____ ____, 20____, and
Ending _____ ____, 20____.

Month-To-Month

Beginning _____ ____, 20____.

(a) JOINT AND SEVERAL TENANCY: If more than one person signs this lease as a Tenant, their obligations are joint and several. **This means that each person is responsible not only for his or her individual obligations, but also for the obligations of all other Tenants.** This includes paying rent and performing all other terms of this lease. A judgment entered against one or more Tenant(s) does not bar an action against the others.

Each Tenant must initial this paragraph:

(1) _____, (2) _____, (3) _____, (4) _____.

(b) RENT: Tenant must pay Landlord, as rent for the entire term, a total of $_____, being $_____each month, beginning _____ ____, 20___, and the same amount on or before the 1st day of each succeeding month. Rent must be paid and all communications must be sent to the Landlord at the following address:

_____

(Street Address, Apartment, City, State, and Zip Code)

(c) DISCOUNTED RENT: If Landlord receives the rent on time, Tenant will be granted a $_____ discount. The discount is meant to encourage prompt payment of rent. Late rent may subject the Tenant to eviction proceedings and liability for damages.

(d) SECURITY DEPOSIT: Tenant must pay Landlord $_____ on _____ ____, 20___, which Landlord holds as a security deposit for Tenant's performance of all the terms of this lease. Unless a cash bond or surety bond is filed with the Secretary of State, the security deposit must be deposited at the following financial institution and may be mingled with the security deposits of Landlord's other tenants:

_____

(Name of Financial Institution,
Street Address, City, State, and Zip Code)

NOTICE:
You must notify your landlord in writing
within 4 days after you move of a
forwarding address where you can be reached
and where you will receive mail;
otherwise your landlord shall be relieved of
sending you an itemized list of damages and the
penalties adherent to that failure.

(e) NONREFUNDABLE CLEANING FEE: Tenant must pay a nonrefundable cleaning fee of $_____ at the beginning of the lease term.

(f) OCCUPANCY: Only the persons who sign this lease may reside at the premises. If more than _____ persons occupy the premises, the Landlord may terminate this tenancy or assess additional rent of $_____ each month for each additional person. **Occupancy must not exceed the number mandated by local ordinance. This premises are licensed for ____ persons.** Tenant may accommodate guests for reasonable periods (up to 2 weeks); other arrangements require Landlord's consent. *Note:* If the premises are located in the City of East Lansing, the occupancy limit must be displayed on the license and posted in the premises. The city may fine violators $500 a day for over-occupancy.

(g) SLEEPING ROOMS: Basements, attics, and other rooms must not be used as sleeping rooms if they do not comply with the local ordinance for windows, minimum square footage, exits, and ventilation. This is meant to protect Tenant's health and safety. **The following areas may not be used as sleeping rooms:**

_____, _____,

_____, _____.

Note: The City of East Lansing may fine violators $509 or they may be sentenced up to 90 days in jail.

(h) KEYS/LOCKS: Tenant will receive _____ keys from the Landlord. On or before the termination of this lease, Tenant must return all keys or Tenant will be charged $_____ for changing the locks. If Tenant loses the keys or gets locked out of the premises, Landlord will provide an extra key to Tenant and may charge Tenant $_____. Tenant must never gain entrance to the premises by force through a window or door, or otherwise without a key. Tenant must not change or add locks without Landlord's written consent.

(i) UNAUTHORIZED USE OF MAILING ADDRESS: Only a Tenant may use the mailing address of the premises. Allowing someone else to use the mailing address will increase the monthly rent $_____.

(j) CONDITION OF PREMISES AT THE BEGINNING OF TENANT'S OCCUPANCY: Tenant acknowledges receipt of two blank copies of an inventory checklist. **Tenant must complete both checklists and return one to the Landlord within 7 days after Tenant takes possession** of the premises. Except for those items specifically noted by the Tenant in detail on the inventory checklist, Tenant accepts the premises, and the appliances and furnishings, in good condition. The inventory checklist is used only to assess damages and is not a warranty or promise by Landlord that any item listed on the checklist, but not present on the premises, will be provided.

(k) APPLIANCES AND OTHER FURNISHINGS PROVIDED: Tenant must not remove or loan any item provided with the premises. Landlord will provide the following checked items:

☐ Stove   ☐ _____   ☐ _____

☐ Refrigerator   ☐ _____   ☐ _____

☐ Dishwasher   ☐ _____   ☐ _____

☐ Washer and Dryer   ☐ _____   ☐ _____

(l) SMOKE DETECTORS: Landlord must install smoke-detection devices as required by law. The premises contain _____ smoke-detection devices, all working satisfactorily. Once the tenancy begins, Tenant must regularly test the detectors to ensure that they are working. Tenant must never remove the battery from the smoke-detection device except when necessary to replace it. Tenant must inform the Landlord immediately, in writing, of any defect or malfunction in its operation.

(m) ALTERATIONS: Tenant must not alter the premises without the Landlord's written consent (e.g., painting, wallpapering, installing locks). Landlord will discuss with Tenant a preferred method of hanging pictures and posters. Tenant is responsible for damage to the walls beyond reasonable wear and tear.

(n) REPAIRS AND MAINTENANCE: Landlord must provide and maintain the premises in a safe, habitable, and fit condition. **Tenant must notify Landlord IMMEDIATELY, BY PHONE at _____ of any gas leaks, electrical problems, water damage, broken appliances, or serious structural damage.** Tenant must notify Landlord, in writing, of all other problems needing repair. Landlord must make all repairs to the premises that, in Landlord's sole judgment, are required by law. Landlord must make every effort to do so within a reasonable time. Whenever repairs are delayed for reasons beyond the Landlord's control, the Tenant's obligations are not affected, nor does any claim accrue to Tenant against the Landlord. Landlord must maintain those things requiring periodic maintenance (e.g., heating, air conditioning, cracked windows).

(o) PIPE-FREEZE PREVENTION: If Tenant plans to be away from the premises for any length of time, **the heat must be left on during the cold season and the windows closed** to avoid broken pipes and water damage.

(p) REPAIRS DUE TO TENANT'S NEGLIGENCE: Damage to the premises caused by Tenant's negligence or Tenant's guest's or invitee's negligence, whether by act or omission, will be repaired by Landlord and charged to the Tenant. Whenever repairs are delayed for reasons beyond Landlord's control,

Tenant's obligations are not affected, nor does any claim accrue to the Tenant against Landlord. Tenant must immediately pay the repair costs as additional rent. If Tenant fails to do so, Landlord may take legal action to recover any unpaid rent.

(q) LANDLORD'S RIGHT OF ENTRY: Landlord, or Landlord's agent, may enter the premises at reasonable times, with _____-hour's notice to the Tenant, to examine, protect, make repairs or alterations, or show prospective renters and purchasers. In emergency situations, Landlord is not required to give Tenant notice. If emergency entry occurs, Landlord must, within 2 days, notify Tenant of the date, time, and reason for the entry.

(r) USE OF THE PREMISES: Tenant must use the premises for private residential purposes only. Tenant must not do any of the following, or allow someone else to do any of the following:

- Harass, annoy, or endanger any other tenant or neighbor, or their guests, or create any excessive noise or public nuisance,

- Do anything to the structure or its surroundings that may be hazardous or that will cause Landlord's insurance to be cancelled or premiums to increase,

- Keep any flammable or explosive materials or any dangerous, hazardous, or toxic substance in or around the premises,

- Deface or damage, or allow another to deface or damage, any part of the premises,

- Change the locks or install any additional locks or bolts without Landlord's written consent,

- Place a waterbed or other heavy article on the premises without Landlord's written consent,

- Pour any commercial anti-clogging agent into the sink or drain that may harm the water pipes, or

- Install any antenna or satellite without Landlord's written consent.

(s) ILLEGAL DRUG USE: Tenant must not violate, or knowingly allow another to violate, federal, state, or local laws regarding the use of controlled substances or the use of alcohol by minors in or around the premises. When aware of a violation of this provision, Landlord will file a formal police report. Landlord may recover possession of the premises by summary proceedings when Tenant holds over the premises for 7 days after service of a written demand for possession for termination of this Lease under this provision.

(t) PETS: Dogs, cats, or other pets are not allowed on the premises without Landlord's written consent. If Landlord's written consent is given, Tenant agrees to pay a nonrefundable pet fee of $_____.

(u) PARKING: Landlord will provide parking for Tenant's automobiles. Tenant must keep the parking area free of all debris. Automobiles must be parked only in assigned areas as follows:

CAR #1_____ (year, make, model, and plate number), belonging to _____ must be parked _____.

CAR #2_____ (year, make, model, and plate number), belonging to _____ must be parked _____.

CAR #3_____ (year, make, model, and plate number), belonging to _____ must be parked _____.

CAR #4_____ (year, make, model, and plate number), belonging to _____ must be parked _____.

(v) MISCELLANEOUS COSTS AND OBLIGATIONS: Check the appropriate box below:

☐ Tenant ☐ Landlord ☐ Not Applicable pays for **electricity.**

☐ Tenant ☐ Landlord ☐ Not Applicable pays for **gas or fuel oil.**

☐ Tenant ☐ Landlord ☐ Not Applicable pays for **water and sewage.**

☐ Tenant ☐ Landlord ☐ Not Applicable pays for **trash removal.**

☐ Tenant ☐ Landlord ☐ Not Applicable must **dispose of all trash by placing in a designated container.**

☐ Tenant ☐ Landlord ☐ Not Applicable must **mow the lawn.**

☐ Tenant ☐ Landlord ☐ Not Applicable must **water the lawn.**

☐ Tenant ☐ Landlord ☐ Not Applicable must **rake the leaves.**

☐ Tenant ☐ Landlord ☐ Not Applicable   must **remove snow and ice from the driveway, parking area, walkway, and steps.**

☐ Tenant ☐ Landlord ☐ Not Applicable   must **change the screens and storm doors as weather dictates.**

☐ Tenant ☐ Landlord ☐ Not Applicable   must _____.

☐ Tenant ☐ Landlord ☐ Not Applicable   must _____.

☐ Tenant ☐ Landlord ☐ Not Applicable   must _____.

☐ Tenant ☐ Landlord ☐ Not Applicable   must _____.

(w) PEACEFUL AND QUIET USE OF PREMISES: In exchange for Tenant's timely payment of rent and performance of all the terms of this lease, Landlord must provide peaceful and quiet use of the premises throughout the tenancy.

(x) SUBLET AND ASSIGNMENT: Tenant must not sublet the premises or assign any interest in this lease without Landlord's written consent (not to be unreasonably withheld). If Landlord gives written consent, Landlord must also provide Tenant with an appropriate sublease form.

(y) RENTER'S INSURANCE: Tenant is strongly advised to carry renters' insurance on his or her personal property (e.g., clothing, furniture, household items). Landlord is not responsible for damage to Tenant's personal property, unless Landlord's negligence or intentional act or omission causes the damage.

(z) LEASE ADDENDUM, RULES, AND REGULATIONS: If the premises are located in the City of East Lansing, the *East Lansing Lease Addendum* must be attached. Additional pages or rules and regulations, **signed by all parties,** are incorporated as part of this Lease, and Landlord must provide copies to the Tenant.

(aa) BREACH OF LEASE AND RIGHT TO RE-ENTER AND REGAIN POSSESSION: If Tenant fails to pay rent or violates any other term of this lease, Landlord may terminate the tenancy, reenter the premises, and regain possession in accordance with the law. If Landlord violates any term of this lease, Tenant may terminate the tenancy.

(bb) CONDITION OF THE PREMISES AT THE END OF TENANT'S OCCUPANCY: At the end of Tenant's occupancy, Landlord must complete a termination inventory checklist to assess damages that Landlord claims were caused by the Tenant. This includes unpaid rent, unpaid utilities, and damages beyond reasonable wear and tear caused by the Tenant or someone under Tenant's control. Tenant may ask to be present when the termination inventory checklist is to be completed. Landlord must mail to the Tenant, within 30 days of Tenant's termination of occupancy, an itemized list of damages claimed for which the security deposit may be used provided, of course, that the Tenant has given a forwarding address.

(cc) END OF LEASE TERM: When the lease term ends, Tenant must promptly **vacate the premises, remove all personal property, and return all keys.** Tenant must **dispose of all trash** and leave the premises clean.

(dd) CHANGES TO THIS LEASE: This lease, and any additional pages or rules and regulations incorporated, contains the entire agreement between Landlord and Tenant; no oral agreement is valid. Changes to the terms of this Lease **must be in writing, signed by all parties.**

(ee) ENFORCEMENT OF LEASE PROVISIONS: Failure to strictly enforce any provision of this lease, by either the Landlord or the Tenant, does not constitute acceptance of a change in its terms. Landlord and Tenant are still obligated to perform as indicated in this lease.

(ff) ADDITIONAL PROVISIONS:

_____

_____

_____

_____

_____

This RESIDENTIAL LEASE AGREEMENT is signed on

_____ _____, 20_____.

**Each person who signs it
acknowledges, by their signature, that
they have read it, understand it, and voluntarily agree to it.
Further, each person is mentally competent
and 18 years or older.**

Landlord's Signature(s): _____

_____

Tenant's Signature(s): _____

_____

_____

_____

This document was drafted as a community-service project
by student residents
under the supervision of clinical faculty at the

MICHIGAN STATE UNIVERSITY-DETROIT
COLLEGE OF LAW,
RENTAL HOUSING CLINIC
541 E. Grand River Avenue, P.O. Box 310
East Lansing, MI 48826
Phone (517) 336-8088, Fax (517) 336-8089
We provide legal services to low-income persons in
Ingham, Eaton, and Clinton counties.
Contributions are appreciated and used
to support our general operations.
The Internal Revenue Service has granted
us §501(c)(3) charitable, tax-exempt status.
Contributions are eligible for the charitable
tax deduction under Internal Revenue Code §170.

GLOSSARY
TALKING THE TALK: SOME REAL-ESTATE TERMS AND CONCEPTS

Much of the language of real estate has a distinctly medieval flavor to it. There's a good reason for this, because the basic conceit of private property, as we think of it in the 21st-century United States, grew up in Britain almost a thousand years ago.

No one reads this kind of real-estate book for a history lesson and few, if any, authors of how-to books make any effort to address the origins of what they are teaching. Who needs it? That's understandable, though unfortunate, for land is the basis of economics, politics and culture. When you get right down to it, many of the high points of human history—and most of the low—have revolved around the acquisition and exploitation of real estate.

Most of our modern real-estate practices can be traced back to William the Conqueror, the Norman king who invaded England in 1066. He made up the basic rules of real estate in order to parcel out the vanquished countryside to his cronies. The king first asserted ownership of all the land and then gave a lot of it away by issuing **grants, titles** or **deeds** to his fellow Normans and to whichever of the local nobles had welcomed his arrival. (You can imagine what happened to the land of the locals who didn't welcome him.)

Six hundred years later, William's and the others' descendants brought England's common law and its considerable body of real-estate customs and practices to North America, driving out the differing property ownership rules of most other European colonists and the native Americans.

Interestingly, the term "real estate" itself has nothing to do with reality, as one might imagine, but everything to do with royalty. *Real* derives from the French *royale* and refers to the king's blanket ownership of the country. Today, of course, the term describes anyone's land and anything that is permanently attached to it. In the United States, we make a distinction between **real property** and **personal property**—your house versus your car, for example. The former is also called **realty** or **immobile property,** the latter **chattel** or **movable property.**

Since land cannot be pocketed like gold or herded like cattle, the king and the **landlords** had to come up with a way of registering property boundaries and recording ownership. The landlords had to know where their **tenants** could farm, cut wood or graze livestock. And the king needed to know how much his **sheriff** (from the Anglo-Saxon "shire-reeve") could collect in taxes from property owners.

In William's day, the king granted only **life estates** to the nobles, which meant that the land reverted to the king upon the death of the landlord. That practice ended in 1290, when the nobles won **freeholds** to property. They then owned the land in **fee simple** (from "fief simple," an unconstrained parcel), which meant that they could then pass their estates on to their heirs or sell their lands to others.

While fee simple is the most fundamental and common form of ownership, it is by no means the only way that one can hold property in the 21st century. There are still life estates, but there is also a similar form of holding called an **estate for years,** which limits ownership to a specified length of time. Similar to that is a **leasehold,** which can last for decades (99-year leaseholds are quite common). Property that has been taken over from a life estate or other limited form of ownership is

WHERE ELSE TO LOOK

There is an excellent glossary online at RealEstateJournal.com (http://www.realestatejournal.com), a Web site of *The Wall Street Journal.* Other on-line glossaries you may find helpful include:

- http://www.citifinancial.com/faq/faqglossary.php

- http://www.crye-leike.com/commercial/glossary.php

- http://www.freddiemac.com/finance/smm/a_f.htm

- http://www.hud.gov/offices/hsg/sfh/buying/glossary.cfm

- http://www.reiclub.com/real-estate-terms.php

In print, I have long relied on definitions in *Barron's Real Estate Handbook* (Barron's Educational Series) and the more handy, though far-less inclusive, *Realty Bluebook,* by Robert de Heer (Dearborn Real Estate Education).

※

said to be a **reversion.** Finally, there are **concurrent** or **cotenancy** holdings that divide ownership of a single piece of property among two or more parties.

We have much the same system as William. His **metes and bounds** property lines based on local man-made and natural landmarks evolved into the more rigidly surveyed town **plat maps** of the early American colonies and, with the **Land Ordinance of 1785,** the six-mile square townships of the **Public Land Survey System** that provided the geographic framework for virtually the entire man-made environment west of the Appalachian Mountains. Today, every county courthouse in the country maintains property records of all the land in the county. Anyone can consult the county maps to learn the boundaries and ownership of every lot of real estate in the county. And in most counties, it's the sheriff's department that is charged with carrying out real-estate-related actions, such as **foreclosures, auctions** and **evictions.**

Potential real-estate investors take note: Even after several centuries of widespread fee-simple ownership, the notion that an owner can do anything he wants with his property has no historical basis. Government—either in the form of the Crown, the state, the town council or, today, even a private neighborhood homeowners' association—has always restricted land uses and asserted limited ownership or usage rights to privately held properties. The medieval king restricted what game could be killed or crops raised. The concept of **eminent domain**— the taking of private land for public use—predates the birth of the United States and is recognized as a power of the state in the Bill of Rights. Other restrictions are expressed in a myriad of fashions—from utility **easements** granting companies rights to string wires over your land or run gas lines under it to **restrictive covenants** dictating everything from what color you can paint your house to whether you can leave a car parked on your driveway overnight. Towns and cities restrict property uses mainly through their **building codes** and **zoning laws,** which lay out acceptable engineering, design and use of properties. The first zoning law in the United States was in New York City in 1916. It was written to preserve sunlight, which was being blocked by the new skyscrapers rising in lower Manhattan.

Today, similar restrictions protect the rugged central coast of California, postcard-quaint New England villages and the 18th-century squares of Savannah. William would do just fine talking the lingo and navigating the modern real-estate world. But there are a few terms he might need some help with.

absorption Mainly a term used in the commercial real-estate business, it refers to the rate at which an area "absorbs" or rents out new space. Absent a great deal of reckless, speculative building, rising absorption pushes the vacancy rate down. It is a good indicator of the overall health of the economy. From the National Association of Realtors: "Net absorption of office space, which includes leasing of new space coming on the market as well as space in existing properties, should rise strongly to 58.0 million square feet [in 2005] and 71.5 million in 2006, up from 45.3 million square feet projected for [2004] and 20.0 million in 2003."

add-on factor   Refers to the money that a landlord receives for unrentable space, such as lobbies, public corridors or restrooms. The landlord adds on the costs of these spaces to tenants' rents. A rental space of 10,000 square feet might actually include an add-on factor of several hundred square feet of common areas.

anchor tenant   A well-known commercial retail business, such as a national chain store or regional department store, that serves as the principal draw at a shopping center or mall.

annual percentage rate (APR)   The actual cost of borrowing money. It will be higher than the quoted interest rate because it includes the interest rate, loan origination fees, loan discount points and other credit costs.

appraisal   An estimate of a property's fair market value. It is typically based on estimates of replacement cost, income or comparable sales of similar properties.

assumable mortgage   Rare in residential real estate, but not so unusual in commercial properties. An assumable mortgage allows the next purchaser of a property to carry on the payments and other obligations of an existing note and mortgage.

balloon loan   Also called a "bullet loan," a balloon loan is amortized over a long period but must be paid in a shorter one, typically resulting in a large final payment due at the end of the loan period. Example: If a note is written for $200,000 at a fixed 6.5 percent rate of interest with payments based on an amortization schedule of 30 years and a balloon payment due in 5 years, the first 59 payments will each be $1,264, and the last payment will be $187,000.

bridge loan   A temporary loan that buyers often use to acquire a property quickly. Most often, buyers use bridge loans to buy a new property while another is being sold.

capitalization rate   The "cap rate" is the most widely used ratio for determining the financial return on an income property. It is expressed as a percentage and figured by dividing the sale price into the net operating income. Example: A $200,000 property with a net operating income of $20,000 would have a cap rate of 10 percent.

cash flow   What's left after you pay all the bills, including all operating expenses and debt payments.

certificate of occupancy   A legal document certifying that a building or apartment has been inspected and is suitable for occupancy. In most places, you can't legally rent a house or apartment without a "C of O."

closing costs   Various outrageous, inexplicable fees and expenses payable by the seller or buyer at the time of a real-estate closing, including but rarely limited to broker commissions, title insurance, lender fees, recording fees, inspection fees, appraisal fees and attorney's fees.

comparable sales   Recent sales of similar properties, which are studied to determine the fair-market value of a property. "Comps," as they are sometimes called, should have as many similarities as possible, including neighborhood, square footage, lot size, construction, room count, floor plan, amenities and traffic patterns.

conforming loan   A loan that conforms to the underwriting guidelines of Fannie Mae (Federal National Mortgage Association), Freddie Mac (Federal Home Loan Mortgage Corporation), the Federal Housing Administration or the Department of Veterans Affairs. In 2005, the conforming loan limit for a single-family property was $359,650, up from $252,700 in 2000. There are other, higher loan limits for multifamily properties. Loans for amounts greater than the conforming limits usually carry a slightly higher interest rate and are called "jumbo loans."

debt-to-income ratio   A lender's gauge of a borrower's ability to make the monthly payments on a loan, based on the percentage of a borrower's monthly pretax income that goes to debt payments.

Lenders typically prefer that borrowers spend no more than 28 percent of their monthly income for housing and 8 percent more on all other debts, but ratios can vary according to the creditworthiness of the borrower and local custom. In high-cost areas, lenders are more likely to allow a higher percentage of income for housing, as much as 40 percent in places such as New York or San Francisco.

Prudent practice: Keep your total housing cost to no more than 25 percent of pretax income.

deed in lieu of foreclosure   A deed surrendered by a borrower to a lender to satisfy a mortgage debt and avoid foreclosure.

deed of trust   A legal feint used in many states in place of a mortgage. While a mortgage is between a borrower and lender, a deed of trust involves a borrower, a lender and a trustee, who holds the property in trust as security for the debt.

deficiency judgment   A judgment sought by a lender who wants to recover any losses on a foreclosure. The ruling grants the lender the difference between the proceeds of a forced sale and the balance remaining on a mortgage debt.

discount points   Interest paid "up front," at the time that a loan is funded, mainly to lower the note rate of the loan and the monthly payment.

Example: A "no-points" $200,000 loan at 6.5 percent for 30 years costs $1,264 month. But if you were willing to pay four points (4 percent, or $8,000) up front, you could get $200,000 for just 5.5 percent and save $128 a month. In this case, the extra up-front cost will be paid back in about 62 months, so you would come out ahead if you own the property for five years.

In contrast, if you use the $8,000 to make a larger down payment and thus a lower beginning balance, you'll save $50 a month for 30 years but pay about $36,000 more in interest due to the higher rate. If you buy $8,000 worth of Treasury bonds, your annual income will be just $336. Best scenario? Pay the discount points and use the $128 to make an additional principal payment each month. You'll pay off the mortgage about 6 years early and save $97,000 in interest.

earnest money   A good-faith deposit. Local practices vary. In some places, you are expected to include an earnest-money check with a written offer; in others, you put up your earnest money after an oral offer has been accepted and a contract has been written. Amounts vary as well. Multimillion-dollar deals have been agreed upon with a handshake and a $50 personal check, while some home sellers may require a certified check for 10 percent of the price.

effective gross income (EGI)   All rents and other income from a property minus an appropriate vacancy factor. Example: A building with 10 rented $1,000-a-month units and a 10 percent vacancy factor would have an EGI of $108,000.

equity participation   A lender claims a share in the gross profits, net profits or net proceeds in the event of a sale or refinance of a property, usually granted in exchange for a lower interest rate or other preferred loan terms.

escalation clause   A provision in a lease that provides for rent increases, either periodically or as a result of increased operating costs.

foreclosure   A procedure by which a lender ("mortgagee") takes title or forces the sale of a borrower's ("mortgagor") property. It's always good to avoid a foreclosure.

And be careful. It's rare, but the IRS can come looking for money after the lender takes over your property. The government can view the wiping out of the loan as what it likes to call a "taxable event." Here's the thinking: If you default on a $100,000 loan, and the lender then sells the property for $80,000, in the eyes of the IRS, you have been forgiven $20,000 of debt. That's income. Uh-oh.

gross leasable area   The floor area that tenants actually occupy and use; the total area that produces rental income.

HVAC   Heating, ventilating and air-conditioning make up a significant portion of the cost of building and operating a property. Indeed, count on the mechanical and electrical portion of a building project to eat up at least 20 percent of a total construction budget.

index   The cost of money that is used to determine the interest rate for an adjustable rate mortgage (ARM). Common indexes (all are published daily in *The Wall Street Journal*) are the prime rate, the London Interbank Offered Rate (LIBOR), the Cost of Funds Index (COFI) and the one-year Treasury bill.

Generally, loans that adjust monthly use the prime rate; loans that adjust semiannually use LIBOR; and loans that adjust annually use the Treasury bill or the Cost of Funds Index. Typically, a margin of about two percentage points is added to the index to set the mortgage rate. So if the one-year Treasury bill is yielding 4.26 percent, as it did at the end of October 2005, an ARM pegged to it would carry a rate of about 6.26 percent.

joint tenancy and **tenants in common**   Two ways to take title of a property by two or more persons. In a joint tenancy, each owner has an "undivided" interest. Married couples usually hold properties as joint tenants, so that either spouse will own the property completely when the other dies. Unrelated business partners, however, are far more likely to own properties as tenants in common, with each partner owning just a portion that is passed on to an estate upon the partner's death.

lease option   A lease that combines a rental agreement with an option agreement that gives the lessee (tenant) the right to purchase the property in the future. A lease option will usually require some additional monthly or annual payment to keep the option in effect.

lease purchase   A lease that combines a rental agreement with a purchase agreement. A tenant will usually pay a fixed amount over the monthly rent that will, over time, add up to a down payment.

legal description   A geographical description identifying a property by survey, metes and bounds, or lot numbers of a recorded plat.

lien   A recorded claim against a property, usually to secure a debt, delinquent taxes or payment for services. Liens must be retired before a property can be sold or its title transferred.

loan-to-value ratio (LTV)   Loan principal divided by the property's appraised value. Typical home loans have an LTV of 80 percent or 90 percent.

market rent   The going rate—rent that a property commands on the open market without rent controls or discounts.

market value   The sale price a property commands in a competitive and open market.

master lease A primary lease that allows but controls sub-leases, as in an office situation in which the master tenant operates a business of renting temporary studio, work or desk space to others.

mortgage French for "dead pledge," a written promise to pay back a loan secured by real estate. Most mortgages are written for 30-year payback or "amortization" periods that require hefty interest payments early in the period and gradually increasing principal payments.

The government subsidizes home mortgage costs via the interest-payment deduction in the income-tax code. Property investors may deduct the full cost of interest from rental income. In either case, however, over the entire length of a 30-year mortgage, interest payments will far outstrip principal payments, so it is always best for a borrower who plans to hold the property for a long time to pay off a mortgage ahead of schedule.

Properties can have multiple mortgages. The principal or senior mortgage on a property is the first mortgage. That's what most homeowners have. A home-equity line of credit is a subordinate—usually a second—mortgage. After the government, the holder of the first mortgage has the first claim on a property in any default. Subordinate mortgages are labeled according to the date of recording as second, third, and so on.

negative amortization A very bad consequence of taking out an adjustable rate mortgage that features exceptionally low interest rates. If a borrower makes just the minimum payment, it may not cover all of the interest that would normally be due. The difference, which is called "deferred interest," is then added to the principal so the balance on the loan grows larger instead of smaller. In a declining real-estate market, this could be devastating because a property owner could end up owing far more on a loan than the property is worth.

nonrecourse loan   A loan in which the lender cannot seek a deficiency judgment against a borrower in default.

operating expenses   Maintenance, repairs, management, utilities, taxes and insurance and other actual costs of operating a building. At tax time, a landlord is likely to have very high operating expenses, but they will shrink into near insignificance when the landlord puts the property up for sale.

PITI   The shorthand way of stating the most usual elements of a residential mortgage payment: *principal, interest, taxes* and *insurance*. When all four are part of the monthly payment, the lender escrows the taxes and insurance and pays them when they come due.

PMI   Private mortgage insurance is required on loans with down payments of less than 20 percent of the purchase price. It protects the interest of lenders, not property owners, in the event of a mortgage default.

quitclaim deed   A short-form deed that passes title to a property, but there is no assurance that the title is valid. Quitclaim deeds frequently are used in divorces to transfer one spouse's property interests to the other. They are also used in real-estate scams, however, to fraudulently convey ownership rights that don't exist.

refinancing   Paying off one loan with another became the national pastime in the first few years of the century, when interest rates hit 40-year lows and real-estate prices hit all-time highs.

The result? "Cash-out" refinancing, in which an owner takes advantage of a property's appreciation, refinances for more money than the previous loan and pockets the difference. Good for investors; foolish for homeowners.

A savvy investor can use cash-out refinancing to realize

some income or to raise investment funds while skirting the tax laws. Example: Refinance a $180,000 loan on a property that's doubled in value, and you will be able to take out $180,000, tax free. (Remember: No negatives. The building must be able to cover the additional monthly mortgage payment.)

When homeowners try this, however, they are saddled with higher monthly payments and new long-term loan commitments. If they use the extra money to invest, they may be OK. But too many homeowners use refinancing proceeds for vacations, cars or other purchases—which they will spend the next 30 years paying for.

rehab Buy it cheap. Clean it up, fix it up, paint it up. Then sell it.

sale-leaseback A deal in which an owner-occupant sells property to an investor. The new owner agrees to lease the property back to the previous owner, who will then occupy the space as a tenant.

There are a number of reasons why an owner might want to make such an arrangement. The original owner may need the cash from the sale or may have used up all the building's depreciation. In either case, the new lease payments will be fully deductible and will reduce the company's potential tax liabilities. The investor is buying guaranteed income while restarting the depreciation clock at a higher base.

Section 8 A federal housing-voucher program through which low-income families can rent or purchase houses or apartments. The program is administered by local public-housing authorities.

Section 1031 The part of the Internal Revenue Code that allows for the tax-free "exchange" of interests in income-producing properties ("property held for productive use in a trade or business or for investment"), called a 1031 exchange. Actually, no swap or exchange is required. You must work through an intermediary to sell and then buy and close on another "like-kind" property within six months.

site development   First-stage "hard improvements" to raw land—grading, utilities, etc.—that must be made before a building can be built.

space, price, location   Pick two. If you want to buy the biggest, fanciest building in the best part of town, the price will be astronomical. If you want to spend less money but stay in the silk-stocking district, you will have to buy a much more modest building. Or you can get a big, fancy building at a really good price in a much-worse neighborhood. You can have the space you want, the price you want or the location you want. Pick two.

tax liens and **tax deeds**   A tax lien is a claim on a property, usually by a state or local government, for delinquent property taxes. All mortgages and other liens are subordinate to a tax lien. That means the government's claim on a property comes before even the holder of the first mortgage and even if the mortgage debt is far greater than the amount of the back taxes. (A tax deed is issued when the government actually seizes a property.)

Here's where investors come in. In most tax-lien states, investors can buy the liens at auction for just the cost of the back taxes and penalties. That transfers the government's claim on the property to the investor. The delinquent property owners are then required to redeem the liens from the investor, usually paying a very high interest rate that is set by the state government. In Colorado, for instance, the variable rate was 14 percent in late 2005; it's a flat 25 percent for six months in Texas.

It's good money, but not easy money. Mortgage holders have a great interest in protecting their positions, so individual investors will likely be bidding for liens and deeds against lenders with deeper pockets. And the vast majority of property owners eventually pay off their back taxes.

But if the property owner fails to retire the tax lien, the investor can take the property. Redemption time periods vary greatly by state—usually from one to five years. And some states even allow delinquent owners to redeem their property after a tax-deed sale. The IRS also acquires and sells properties for unpaid taxes.

title insurance Like PMI (private mortgage insurance), title insurance is a protection for lenders that property owners pay for. Title companies conduct title searches and then issue expensive policies insuring against loss resulting from defects of title or claims or liens related to a specific property. Lenders usually require a new title-insurance policy each time a property changes hands or is refinanced.

The title-insurance business originated in the United States in the 19th century, when county-by-county property records could be difficult to obtain or verify, but its great growth period came in the mid-20th century with the government-backed mortgages that fueled the suburban home-building boom.

Title companies have long justified their existence and fees because of the extensive research they must do for each policy. The argument has become less convincing, however, as title companies have merged and consolidated their property databases and as most public records have been computerized and, increasingly, become available to anyone with an Internet connection.

turnkey project A project in which a developer or general contractor completes the building; also, the construction of ten-

ant improvements to the specific requirements of the future
owner or tenant.

vacancy factor   The amount of gross revenue that is lost or is
expected to be lost because of vacancies—usually expressed as
a percentage of rentable square footage or, in residential projects, of rentable units.

BIBLIOGRAPHY

Like the rest of this book, this list of books and Web sites is not meant to be an exhaustive compilation. In addition to the sources cited in the main text, these represent the published materials that I found myself most frequently visiting to check and double-check facts, figures and insights.

There are scores of very good, useful sources that I have not included and hundreds, if not thousands, of not-so-good ones that I haven't listed, either. I have arranged these in a Good-Better-Best arrangement to give you some idea of what I found to be most useful for this presentation.

Having now written this book, I appreciate the time, energy and effort that these and others have put into their works, and I appreciate and acknowledge the help that each and every one of these authors has given me.

BOOKS

BEST

Berges, Steve. *The Complete Guide to Buying and Selling Apartment Buildings.* 2nd ed. John Wiley & Sons, 2005.

———. *The Complete Guide to Real Estate Finance for Investment Properties.* John Wiley & Sons, 2004.

Eldred, Gary W. *The Beginner's Guide to Real Estate Investing.* John Wiley & Sons, 2004.

Fishman, Stephen. *Every Landlord's Tax Deduction Guide.* Nolo Press, 2005.

Hoven, Vernon. *The Real Estate Investor's Tax Guide.* 4th ed. Dearborn Real Estate Education, 2003.

McLean, Andrew, and Gary W. Eldred. *Investing in Real Estate.* 4th ed. John Wiley & Sons, 2003.

Reed, John T. *How to Get Started in Real Estate Investment.* John T. Reed, 2000.

Rider, Stuart Leland. *The Complete Idiot's Guide to Real Estate Investing.* 2nd ed. Alpha Books, 2003.

Robinson, Leigh. *Landlording.* 9th ed. ExPress, 2004.

Stewart, Patricia, Ralph Warner, and Janet Portman. *Every Landlord's Legal Guide.* 7th ed. Nolo Press, 2004.

BETTER

Edwards, Brian F., Casey Edwards, and Susannah Craig-Edwards. *The Complete Idiot's Guide to Making Money with Rental Properties.* 2nd ed. Alpha Books, 2004.

Holton, Lisa. *The Essential Dictionary of Real Estate.* Barnes & Noble Books, 2004.

Lereah, David. *Are You Missing the Real Estate Boom?* Currency-Doubleday, 2005.

Talbott, John. *The Coming Crash in the Housing Market.* McGraw-Hill, 2003.

GOOD

Andrew, Douglas R. *Missed Fortune 101.* Warner Business Books, 2005.

Dulworth, Mike, and Teresa Goodwin. *Renovate to Riches.* John Wiley & Sons, 2004.

Hall, Craig. *Timing the Real Estate Market.* McGraw-Hill, 2004.

Hill, Robert J. *What No One Ever Tells You About Investing in Real Estate.* Dearborn Trade Publishing, 2005.

Irwin, Robert. *How to Get Started in Real Estate Investing.* McGraw-Hill, 2002.

Keller, Gary, with David Jenks and Jay Papasan. *The Millionaire Real Estate Investor.* McGraw-Hill, 2005.

McElroy, Ken. *The ABC's of Real Estate Investing.* Warner Business Books, 2004.

Rejnis, Ruth, and Calire Walter. *Buying Your Vacation Home for Fun & Profit*. Real Estate Education Co. (Dearborn Financial Publishing), 1996.

Ross, George H., with Andrew James McLean. *Trump Strategies for Real Estate*. John Wiley & Sons, 2005.

Walker, June. *Self-Employed Tax Solutions*. Globe Pequot Press, 2005.

Williamson, Richard T. *Selling Real Estate Without Paying Taxes*. Dearborn Trade Publishing, 2003.

WEB SITES

BEST

Bankrate.com: http://www.bankrate.com

Bizspace: http://www.bizjournals.com/bizspace

The Creative Investor: http://www.thecreativeinvestor.com

Department of Housing and Urban Development: http://www.hud.gov

Dinkytown: http://www.dinkytown.net

Ernst & Young Real Estate:
http://www.ey.com/global/content.nsf/US/Real_Estate_-_Overview

Fairmark.com *Tax Guide for Investors:* http://www.fairmark.com/index.html

Fannie Mae: http://www.fanniemae.com

Federation of Exchange Accommodators: http://www.1031.org

Financial Services Fact Book:
http://www.financialservicesfacts.org/financial2

Freddie Mac: http://www.freddiemac.com

Internal Revenue Service: http://www.irs.gov

Instructions for Form 8582-CR: http://www.irs.gov/instructions/i8582cr

IRS Glossary: http://www.irs.gov/app/understandingTaxes/jsp/tools_glossary.jsp

Passive Activity Loss Audit Technique Guide: http://www.irs.gov/businesses/small/article/0,,id=146318,00.html

Publication 527: http://www.irs.gov/publications/p527/ar02.html#d0e4189

Publication 544: http://www.irs.gov/publications/p544/ch02.html#d0e3841

Publication 925: http://www.irs.gov/pub/irs-pdf/p925.pdf

Real Estate Links: http://www.irs.gov/businesses/small/industries/content/0,,id=99080,00.html

Jack Brause Real Estate Library (New York University): http://www.nyu.edu/library/rei/brweb.htm

Landlord.com: http://www.landlord.com

Loopnet: http://www.loopnet.com

Morningstar: http://www.morningstar.com

National Association of Realtors: http://www.realtor.org

National Association of Real Estate Investment Trusts: http://www.nareit.com

Invest in REITs: http://www.investinreits.com/index.cfm

Portfolio magazine: http://www.nareit.com/portfoliomag

Nolo Press: http://www.nolo.com

Real Estate Journal (*The Wall Street Journal*): http://www.realestate-journal.com

Urban Land Institute: http://www.uli.org

BETTER

Adjusters Group LLC: http://adjustersgroup.com

The Bond Market Association: http://www.investinginbonds.com

Building-Cost.net: http://www.building-cost.net

Campbell R. Harvey's Finance Glossary: http://www.duke.edu/~charvey/Classes/wpg/glossary.htm

Case Schiller Weiss: http://www.cswv.com

Center for Real Estate Studies: http://www.indiana.edu/~cres/realestate/?q=

C-loans.com: http://www.c-loans.com/

Commercial Investment Real Estate: http://ciremagazine.com

Curbed: http://www.curbed.com

Economics and Statistics Administration (Department of Commerce): https://www.esa.doc.gov

Everything RE: http://www.everythingre.com

Fidelity Mortgage-Backed Securities: http://personal.fidelity.com/products/fixedincome

GE Commercial Finance: http://www.cefcorp.com/baf/index.asp

GMAC Commercial Mortgage: http://www.gmaccm.com

Guidant Financial Group: http://www.guidantfinancial.com

Home Pages: http://www.homepages.com

Ilyce Glink: http://www.thinkglink.com/

Inman News: http://www.inman.com/

Investopedia: http://www.investopedia.com

John T. Reed: http://www.johntreed.com

Money magazine real estate: http://money.cnn.com/real_estate/

Mortgage 101: http://www.mortgage101.com

Mr. Landlord: http://www.mrlandlord.com

National Apartment Association: http://www.naahq.org

Real Estate Investors of Nashville: http://www.reintn.net

Real Estate Owner: http://www.real-estate-owner.com

Realty Times: http://realtytimes.com

REIClub.com: http://www.reiclub.com

Rental Housing Online: http://rhol.org/

Retail Traffic: http://retailtrafficmag.com

RS Means (Reed Construction Data): http://www.rsmeans.com

Tax Foundation: http://www.taxfoundation.org

Zell/Lurie Real Estate Center at Wharton: http://
     realestate.wharton.upenn.edu/

Good

BOMA (Building Owners and Managers Association) International:
     http://www.boma.org

BuyIncomeProperties.com: http://www.buyincomeproperties.com

Chattel Appraisals: http://www.chattelappraisals.com

Condo Flip: http://www.condoflip.com

Institute of Real Estate Management: http://www.irem.org

International Real Estate Digest: http://www.ired.com

John Schaub: http://www.johnschaub.com

Landlord Association: http://www.landlordassociation.org

National Real Estate Investor: http://www.nreionline.com

National Real Estate Investors Association: http://
     www.nationalreia.com

Pikenet: http://www.pikenet.com

Real Estate Tax Issues for Homeowners: http://
    www.real-estate-owner.com
RealEstateZoo.com: http://realestatezoo.com
RentLaw.com: http://www.rentlaw.com
Tax Lien Certificates: http://www.tax-lien-certificates.com/
Tax Loopholes: http://www.taxloopholes.com
Tax Topics: http://taxtopics.net

ACKNOWLEDGMENTS

In addition to all the persons quoted in the text who shared their time, expertise and stories to help me write this book, it could not have been produced without the help of dozens of others.

My *Wall Street Journal* boss, Larry Rout, let me take the time I needed away from the office but also endured and improved at least three versions of the manuscript.

My greatest professional debt is to the staff of *The Wall Street Journal Sunday*. On many days, Brian Cronk, Karen Damato, Gay Miller, Mark Tyner and the others let me perform my minimal editor's duties as a mere disembodied voice on the phone or writer of e-mails.

At the daily *Journal* and WSJ Books: Thanks to Paul Steiger, Jim Pensiero, Fred Kempe, Ken Wells and the indomitable Roe D'Angelo for giving me the assignment and getting me through the publishing process. At Crown: John Mahaney and Lindsay Orman.

Andrew Blackman and Raymund Flandez did a lot of the heavy lifting—from finding and interviewing some of the landlords to proofreading and fact checking. They also helped rope in Kevin McKay and others at the *Journal*'s Market Data Group.

My colleagues Tom Herman, Glenn Ruffenach and Jay Hershey read versions of various chapters and provided advice and encouragement. Dave Kansas and Jeff Opdyke, whose own books in this series preceded this one, served as much appreciated guides and trailblazers. My good friends David Cay Johnston and Ed Sallee (and his associate Kathi Preuit), along with my brother Leonard, read portions of the book and offered their helpful insights. I owe a special debt to Alan Kadet and Eugene Zappi, who, quite literally, managed to keep me together through the writing.

I can't even begin to thank—or name—all of the friends, family members, business associates and acquaintances who over the years taught me about real estate, though none educated me quite so much as did my parents, Leonard and Doris Crook. They never shied from drafting their sons in projects ranging from managing a rental property to gutting and rehabbing houses.

Finally, there's Jamie and Lauren, who tolerate my real-estate obsession. I love you both. Jamie, thanks for always picking me up the latest copy of the *Real Estate Book* from the stand at the supermarket. And Lauren, whose first novel, *It's About Your Husband,* beat this book to the stores by two months, I am always your biggest fan. World enough and time.

INDEX

ABOUT THE AUTHOR

DAVID CROOK is the editor of *The Wall Street Journal Sunday,* the 10-million circulation personal-finance section that appears in more than 75 newspapers around the country. He designed and launched the *WSJ Sunday* in 1999, after working on the original team that developed and started the successful "Weekend Journal" section of the daily *Wall Street Journal.* Prior to that, David developed "Home Front" and "Property Report," the paper's residential and commercial real-estate sections.

Before he joined the *Journal* in 1995, David was a reporter and editor at the *Los Angeles Times* and managing editor of a chain of suburban newspapers in Southern California. He and his family live in New York City and Litchfield County, Connecticut.

ALSO FROM *THE WALL STREET JOURNAL.*

GET YOUR FINANCIAL
LIFE IN ORDER WITH
THE MOST TRUSTED
NAME IN THE WORLD
OF FINANCE.

Up-to-date and expertly written, *The Wall Street Journal. Complete Money & Investing Guidebook* provides investors with a simple—but not simplistic—grounding in the world of finance.

The Wall Street Journal. Complete Money and Investing Guidebook

978-0-307-23699-9
$14.95 paper (Canada: $21.00)

The quintessential primer on understanding and managing your money, this indispensable book takes the mystery out of personal finance.

*The Wall Street Journal.
Complete Personal Finance Guidebook*

978-0-307-33600-2
$14.95 paper (Canada: $21.00)

This hands-on, interactive guide to managing your personal finances makes it quick and easy to get your financial life in order and ultimately build wealth.

The Wall Street Journal.
Personal Finance Workbook

978-0-307-33601-9
$13.95 paper (Canada: $21.00)

The Wall Street Journal. Complete Identity Theft Guidebook is the essential guide to both safeguarding your identity and undoing the damage done by identity theft.

The Wall Street Journal.
Complete Identity Theft Guidebook

978-0-307-33853-2
$13.95 paper (Canada: $17.95)

In *The Wall Street Journal. Complete Retirement Guidebook,* you'll learn how to tailor a financial plan for a retirement that could very well be the best part of your life.

The Wall Street Journal.
Complete Retirement Guidebook

978-0-307-35099-2
$14.95 paper (Canada: $19.95)

AVAILABLE FROM THREE RIVERS PRESS WHEREVER BOOKS ARE SOLD.